To John,
Some of these stories
fit into the "fish story" cat...
You'll spot them!

Jim Simmons
11-14-99

Notes to my Friends

Jim Kincaid

Notes to my Friends

Jim Kincaid

Foreword by Ted Koppel

Donning
Norfolk/Virginia Beach

Copyright© 1982 by Jim Kincaid

All rights reserved, including the right to reproduce this book in any form whatsoever without permission in writing from the publisher, except for brief passages in connection with a review. For information, write:
The Donning Company/Publishers
5659 Virginia Beach Boulevard
Norfolk, Virginia 23502.

Library of Congress Cataloging in Publications Data

Kincaid, Jim, 1934-
 Notes to my friends.

 1. Anecdotes. I. Title.
PN6261.K44   818'.5402   82-5031
ISBN 0-89865-208-1   AACR2

Printed in the United States of America.

I've long held the theory that life is a series of accidents. Mine has been.

But if I had the chance to sit down and design a perfect accident, a happy accident, it would not differ essentially from the one that blended my life with Elam and Tidewater.

The original idea was to find a job that would support the dubious investment in Elam.

I found that, but oh what a bonus came with it.

From the first day I went on the air at WVEC-TV the people of the cities and towns within our broadcast radius started making me feel welcome.

I have a deskful of letters and Christmas cards and Valentines and pictures of dogs they've sent me. I've been invited to their homes, to speak to their clubs, to judge or ride in their parades; and the curious thing is, they always wind up thanking me, when it should be the other way around.

Some have been critical, but I can't think of a single mean-spirited attack. And they compliment me in so many ways, I've run out of adequate words to express my appreciation.

Therefore, I would like to dedicate this book to my wife Catherine who believed it possible, to Tom Chisman, my friend, who made it possible, and to the people of Tidewater, who made it worthwhile.

TABLE OF CONTENTS

Page

Foreword
    By Ted Koppel 1
Introduction
    By Tom Chisman 3
Preface
    It's All Betty Jo's Fault 9
Chapter 1
    Looking Back 25
Chapter 2
    An Innocent Abroad In The Economy 31
Chapter 3
    "They Ought Not To Be Doing That" 40
Chapter 4
    The Endless Election Year 53
Chapter 5
    But I Wouldn't Want To Live There 70
Chapter 6
    All Held Hostage 77
Chapter 7
    Little Things Mean A Lot 88
Chapter 8
    At Random 115
Chapter 9
    But Once A Year 128
Chapter 10
    To Saunter Or To Amble 136
Chapter 11
    Down Home 145
Chapter 12
    Looking Ahead 152

FOREWORD
by Ted Koppel

As I remember it, I was about seven. Spencer was about seven, too. He would recall later that I had brought the matches from our kitchen, I was equally sure that he'd brought them from his house; but then we were both under a lot of pressure.

We had started a small fire in a field behind my house. Which is to say, it was a small fire when we started it, but it didn't stay small for long. It had been a very dry summer. The field burned out of control; certainly out of our control. The firemen, fortunately, managed to put out the fire before it did any real damage, although that was purely hearsay to Spencer and me.

By the time the firemen started battling our fire, Spencer and I were hiding in his parents' garage. That's where my mother found us to tell us about the fire and the fire engines and the firemen. My mother thought we might want to see them. She was wrong. She was also immediately suspicious of our disinterest. In fact, I was always convinced that she knew immediately how that fire had started.

All of this, of course, happened a very long time ago, very far from Washington, D.C., where I now work. That isolated instance of pyromania took place in a suburb of London, England back in the late 1940s. Yet somehow, reading Jim's recollections of Arkansas and his childhood, I was struck more by the similarity than the vast difference in our backgrounds. I imagine our mothers might have had some difficulty in understanding one another, separated as they were (as Churchill once noted in a different context) by a common language; but their theories of child-rearing don't seem all that different.

So, it's perhaps not too surprising that Jim Kincaid from Arkansas and Ted Koppel from London should end up in Viet Nam together, and then in Hong Kong together, and later in Washington together. Somehow the separate cauldrons that produced us turned us into observers rather than doers; and there was a lot to observe in Viet Nam and Hong Kong back then. Wasington, it goes without saying, is an endless source of fascination for observers.

1

But then, a few years ago, Jim did something very sensible. He picked himself a beautiful Virginia community, settled down there and began writing a book in the only painless way that a book can be written: unintentionally.

Jim never did have a lick o' sense. He doesn't know that books are not written in dozens of unrelated pieces. He doesn't seem to care that journalists are, by definition, humorless; and how he could have thought that a kid from London would write an introduction to a collection of winsome essays by a contemporary from Arkansas....

Read on. It does get better. Honest.

INTRODUCTION

I knew the voice, and my memory quickly reconstructed the face. He was a relatively small man with a rugged complexion and a smile which you'd have to say was a wry grin. It was Jim Kincaid standing just inside my office door.

We shook hands, a firm friendly grip, and, yes, he'd like a cup of coffee. While it was being prepared, we exchanged small talk about the weather and his drive from Elam. Exactly where was Elam? He needed a map. He said it was between Pamplin and Prospect. My map seemed to indicate it was between Pamplin and Tuggle. Anyway, we agreed it was not too far away—close to Farmville.

It's never wise to hire anyone without at least doing some background investigation—and I'd done just that. We had talked on the phone, and I had followed up by talking with the president of ABC News, Elmer Lower; the then-anchorman, Howard K. Smith; the to-be anchorman, Frank Reynolds; news producer Bill Lord; and Sam Donaldson and other correspondents who had worked with Jim. Kincaid came through with excellent recommendations. Oh, yes, a couple of them said, "He does enjoy a drink now and then." "Every now and then" I knew was not, in newsmen's parlance, exactly infrequently. I must remember that, I thought, as we talked.

He could have stayed with the network. He could have worked in Washington. He had been offered jobs in Richmond, Roanoke, Lynchburg, Greensboro. He really didn't like any of these offers. Norfolk, he said, and WVEC Television looked right to him. So the conversation went to his family. Yes he'd live in Norfolk with Catherine, his wife, and Caroline, his teenage daughter. Were the schools any good in Norfolk? My reply was a positive one, although I'd never been in a Norfolk school. He'd drive to Elam on weekends.

What did I expect from him? Anchor the five-thirty and eleven o'clock news...give them a flair, a lift, a professional touch, and try to teach some of our young reporters that there's no glamour in news. It's hard work...a lot of responsibility...be right rather than first. Agreed. He had the experience and he liked young people since he was not too far from that state himself.

Now the question: "Do you still drink?" No hesitation on

3

his part. "Not any more." I was satisfied on this score. (Two months later, after our news department almost made a clean sweep of the Virginia Associated Press Television awards, I learned that he had attended the awards dinner and had imbibed sufficiently to be noticed. I queried him on this, and a sly grin crept across the corners of his mouth. He straightforwardly told me his earlier reply on drinking was meant to mean "not any more than he used to." You have to be careful how you phrase your questions to Jim Kincaid.)

Then we moved to money. He says he knows what we were both thinking. I was thinking I'd get him for less than he'd ever earned before. He was thinking I'd have to pay him more than I'd ever paid a newsman before. Later he would say we were both right.

We shook hands and that was it. I've never been more fortunate.

Today Jim Kincaid is the most respected newscaster in the area. His speaking talents are in great demand. He could be out every night making speeches if we'd let him. He's gone from North Carolina to the Eastern Shore and most of the cities and towns in between. This year he was invited to make eight commencement speeches. He lectures for police departments on how they should treat the press—and how the press should treat them.

Jim is almost everything you'd want in a newsman, embodying a healthy respect for the tremendous responsibility he has in reporting news; just the right amount of ego; a keen judge of what is news—all the elements which make him a true professional.

We've been together for over four years. I've listened to the tales of his Uncle Otto, the stern grammar lessons from his high school teacher, what Catherine's father paints, his dogs and cats, and . . . we've swapped stories which will never appear in any book. We both chain smoke pipes, and if you see him with his pipe please remind him to switch it to the right corner of his mouth.

The comments he writes are his own contrivances and his cross. His associates at ABC and CBS think he's insane to try to write two commentaries a day, five days a week. He does it—and does it well. I hope the cross does not become too burdensome, for if it does, we'll all be left with just the news—and that's really not enough.

Jim Kincaid...a simple yet complex man who expresses his philosophy so adequately on the air and in this book.

                Thomas P. Chisman
                President & General Manager
                WVEC Television
                Hampton-Norfolk, Virginia
                February 1982

(Woof!)
— Murphy
9/1/82

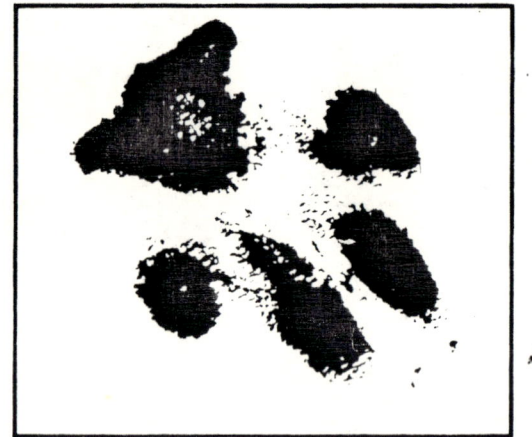

Best Wishes

Notes to my Friends

Jim Kincaid

PREFACE

It's all Betty Jo's fault. Started work, for money, at the age of fourteen. Earlier, actually, if you count the lawns mowed, cows milked, barns cleaned, vegetable rows hoed and watered, and all the then unpleasant, now delightful to remember things a boy is heir to on an Arkansas hill country farm.

But at fourteen we moved to town. A town called Russellville, all of eighteen miles from the farm, and thriving with commerce and jobs for money. A lovely town, maybe eight thousand, and they were folks; folks in the true southern meaning, as mean and good and hateful and pure and varied as those on any block in the Bronx.

Except for the three or four blocks of downtown, Main Street, Commerce and their intersecting streets, Russellville must have been pretty nearly invisible from the air. But since few planes flew over, it probably didn't matter.

In the residential areas, trees of great age lined the streets, turning them into cool tunnels, grey walled and green roofed, and quiet save for the sounds made by dogs and insects and distant freight trains. Oh, had I only known how very lovely it was.

Had a lot of jobs in Russellville; odd jobs, clerk in Cowan-Goodwins Men's Store several Christmas seasons in a row. Soda jerk and short-order cook at Al's Drive-In. Usher, popcorn popper and concession stand operator at the Ritz Theatre. And then to journalism, printer's devil for Craig Lovesey at the *Weekly Tribune,* made forty-five cents an hour, planned marriage... I was seventeen by then.

A "printer's devil" by the way, was a fellow who did those jobs around a printing plant that were below the station of "real" printers. It is my belief that a young man could learn why such persons were called "devils" in his first two hours on the job. The "devil" was the character in the phrase "that poor devil," not the devil in "mean as the devil."

They say printer's ink gets in your blood. It got mostly in my hair and under my nails... but it was darn near as hard to get out as the kind that gets in your blood.

Maybe I should explain Betty Jo. We were a real thing. Her parents were Baptists and hated the very thought of their daughter going with a Catholic; and I had a 1941 Plymouth, and that was my appeal for her. She was redheaded and "built" beyond her years, and that was her appeal for me.

While Betty Jo did manage to survive our three years of intense courtship morally intact, she returned the favor by getting me into a fix. A fix that's lasted more than a quarter of a century. She got me into broadcasting. She was my "steady," and she did that to me.

There was this drive-in restaurant near the high school where she made straight "A's" and I visited occasionally, and Betty and I used to park my old Plymouth under some trees in the back corner of the service area of that drive-in and "court." How long since you heard that word? Well, that's what we called it then, though our parents would probably have called it "petting" and despaired for our souls if they'd seen what went on. They knew, of course, but refused to believe that our morals were, in these tender years, just about what theirs had been in their youth, or for that matter, in Aristotle's. Betty's and mine turned out to be better. She didn't get pregnant, and I didn't either. [In that day, in that part of the country, when one half of a pair of "steadies" got pregnant, everybody was pregnant, even to the most distant uncle or aunt in either family.] But it wasn't fear of pregnancy that kept us pure. It was our "morals." We just "courted," we didn't "make out."

Anyway, during our courting sessions at the drive-in, Betty told me frequently that I had a beautiful voice. And since we had sworn our undying love for each other, I saw no reason to doubt her. She would usually follow up such assertions with a suggestion that I go out to KXRJ (Russellville's only radio station) and ask for a job. I would accept the compliment, reject the suggestion as being an impossible dream, and continue to ply her with compliments and caresses.

"Courting," you see, was a very ritualistic affair in that region, and in among all the groping and kissing and endless recitations of eternal faithfulness and immediate suicide if ever either should leave the other, there were plans for the future. "Steady dating" was what passed for engagement when one was too young to tell one's parents that one planned to marry and/or too poor to buy even the cheapest diamond. And so, we made plans. It wasn't the best part of courting, but an essential part, and held sway because it was the honorable and only route to marital bliss. We often talked about marriage, the house we'd have, babies, how our parents would give us some furniture, how I would swipe enough parts from the junkyard to keep the old Plymouth running, and how I'd make the living.

It was accepted in our society that girls made good grades in school, graduated, got married, had kids, and kept house. Boys, on the other hand, could respectably make barely passing grades, loaf around in pool halls, learn to identify any car by its grillwork, smoke cigarettes and drink cheap whisky, and grow up to be responsible, wage-earning fathers. No one, except preachers, ever questioned these values, and even the preachers only did it because that's the way they made their living.

So, with a living wage the only key to getting between the sheets, Betty and I talked about the future. I figured I could go on holding down several jobs at a time and make as much as forty dollars a week, an ample wage, a generous income. But Betty's vision foresaw a day when that might not be enough, that we might need sixty-five or seventy-five dollars a week.

Sometime after we had been "courting" for more than two years, Betty's hopes for my future had a boost from fate. The English class I sometimes attended and invariably failed, had a competition to choose an "announcer" for a local radio program to be entitled, inspiringly, "News and Views from RHS." I entered the contest, buoyed by the certainty that I would not win, place, or show, thinking that I must be extremely favored by God to have such an opportunity to lay this whole broadcasting fixation of hers to rest. But I won. God, apparently, found my case wanting.

Still, my hopes for the future remained intact. The program consisted of one fifteen-minute period each Saturday morning with me, the announcer, reading what was alleged to be the week's news from the high school. It was so dull, so totally uninformative, so...so high school that any threat of a career in radio seemed remote indeed. I failed, however, to reckon with Betty Jo, God, and Russ Horne.

Betty Jo prayed. I told you she was a Baptist, and they're given to that practice. She prayed for me to get a good job: one that had a future. And God, since he wasn't hearing anything to the contrary from me, listened to Betty Jo, and got Russ Horne to listen to me. Russ, as it happens, owned the radio station and was currently in need of someone who could read

11

aloud for a dollar an hour. Thus, I fit the bill for Betty Jo, God, and Russ Horne. I don't think Russ prayed, or was even aware that he'd been hustled into a divine plan by God and a redheaded, well-constructed, teenaged girl, but he hired me.

There are those who will say that I could have turned down the permanent job Russ offered, but they would be wrong. Times were different then. Young boys did not dispute the wisdom that flowed from older, fully grown men. Such men were to be listened to, and their counsel followed. Such men were powerful and could drink bonded whiskey, even in a dry county. One did not discuss things with such men. One listened, trembled, and obeyed.

Russ Horne was standing there one day after I had plied the public with "News and Views from RHS." "Jim," he said, with an attitude resembling that of a used car salesman who knows the innermost secrets of your soul and pocketbook, "I want you to come to work for me." The absence of a negative response was my entire end of the contract. "I'll be paying you a dollar an hour," came the verdict, "Have your a___out here at 5:30 in the morning for sign-on, and Bill McKenny'll show you what to do." Then came a lecture on broadcast ethics. "Don't drink or cuss in the damn studio." Negotiations complete... what a genius that man had for compression.

Distressed is not the word. I was flooded with a mixture of elation, fear and confusion. On one hand, in just seconds, my possibilities for marital bliss with Betty Jo had increased a hundredfold. On the other hand, dreams of being an auto mechanic, archeologist or pool hustler were at best deferred. My new occupation would leave no time for the constant study and devotion these former dreams required for realization. Well, maybe archeology ... but, visions of Betty Jo tempered the sadness.

I remember leaving the radio station (located on the edge of town on the campus of Arkansas Tech) prepared to live this new life to the fullest. My old Plymouth was parked just next to Russ Horne's late-model Buick, and since I did not want him to suffer the humiliation of having an employee of his stranded for want of gasoline, I took a siphon and collected a three-gallon pre-enlistment bonus. That act raised him considerably in my estimation, since he clearly used premium gasoline. (There is a marked difference in taste when you suck on the hose to get the siphon started; premium is fruitier than regular.) It always pleasured me considerably to find a man to whom the quality in unseen things was important. Russ, obviously was such a man. Working for such a person was a compliment of sorts, since he obviously saw qualities in me that had escaped my teachers and the local constable. I recall debating whether I should give him all my gasoline business, but decided finally that it might be undemocratic or dangerous...or both. I decided not even to discuss it with him.

Filled with the taste of premium gasoline and moral victory, I nursed my Plymouth into life and set off to see Betty Jo and tell her the news. I hasten to add that I did not then know about her deal with God, and I don't think Russ Horne did either. My purpose was to tell her that I did it on my own, purposely, so that she and I could have a secure future and "go all the way." I may even have nurtured a dark hope that we could mutually decide that things were so well set that we might as well go ahead and enjoy what would soon be our legal rights anyway. However, on that particular Saturday, Betty Jo remained chaste. I did describe to her in full detail how I had marched right up to Russ Horne, offered my services, and demanded the unheard of sum of a dollar an hour. She seemed impressed, or I should say, feigned being impressed, and I suppose I missed her wink at God.

Some say I should blame the whole mess on God. But I don't. It was Betty Jo, pure and simple. And now, twenty-five years later I'm stuck with the results. Because of her, I never got around to applying for a job, but just got applied to one. And all for the sake of a possible future toss in the hay.

After KXRJ the pattern was established. In another town about thirty miles from Russellville there was another 250-watt local radio station called KVOM, and it was owned by one JayCee Willis, and his credentials in the persuasive art were something like Russ Horne's only better. Besides, Morrillton was in a "wet" county and my old Plymouth knew the way. J. C. got me to come to work for him for what appeared to be more money, sixty-five dollars a week. However, since J. C. allowed me to work sixty-five hours a week, it all evened out ... for J. C. I don't recall exactly how the deal was made, but I dropped by KVOM one day and his lovely black-haired daughter was there. I took the job (again, it was not offered but ordained) and never got within a hundred yards of her again. J. C.'s grasp of teenage moral values was quite well developed.

It was while pursuing my trade in Morrillton that Betty

Jo and I began to grow apart. Partly because her parents shipped her off to a college in Texas after she graduated from high school, and partly for a host of other reasons. We saw each other from time to time, wrote passionate letters, and continued to swear eternal and singular devotion. But since it took all I could earn to keep a room and the old Plymouth in repair, the goal of marriage and legal sex remained distant. For Betty, it was a simple matter to redirect her life. For me, a pattern had been set that has remained unbreakable to this day. I kept on and on getting jobs without asking for them. If the pattern holds, everything will be all right.

From KVOM in Morrillton it was on to KTHS in Little Rock. More money, it sounded like, and a fifty-thousand-watt clear channel station that could be heard in twenty-seven states. Fellow named B. G. Robertson heard me on KVOM and hired me on the phone. I say hired ... ordered me to come to work for him.

Sometime later an Iowa station that was about to fold under the supervision of one Alex Chesley needed an announcer. Guess who got tapped? Chesley folded and I was about to go back to Arkansas when Jim Conroy of KBIZ KTVO in Ottumwa drafted me. Fate let me be for about a year and then the U. S. Army really drafted me.

The way it happened, it appeared that I volunteered. But I was drafted, and no mistake about it.

Back when I got out of high school I had registered for the draft, but I decided to fox them and volunteer, and thus get the obligation behind me. There was never any question that it was an obligation. The same moral values applied as those that kept Betty Jo and me from extra-marital bliss.

But Betty Jo's deal with God apparently ruled out military service because I applied to the Marine Corps, the Navy and the Army ... in that order ... and was turned down. In that order.

The nation, it seemed, was not hiring.

So, I figured I was off the hook, honorably. What the nation was waiting for was for me to get settled into the idea of being a civilian. In 1957 I had finally done that. I had charge accounts and a new car and an income that seemed sufficient to keep up with them.

Then came the telegram from Uncle Sam. Next thing I knew I had turned my head and coughed, and raised my right hand.

At that point, Betty Jo's deal with the Almighty came into effect again, and I was assigned to a broadcasting job with the American Forces Network in Germany. Not, however, before a delightful period in basic training at Fort Chaffee, Arkansas, where I learned that being a "printer's devil" is a relatively luxurious way of life.

It was during this period that I was given the option of signing up for an extra year for the privilege of working in the "field of my choice," or remaining a draftee and spending the next two years chained to an artillery piece.

Three years later I was passing through Little Rock and B. G. Robertson spotted me and nailed me again. I languished at KTHS awhile and was summoned to New Orleans to meet Bob Guy, program director of WWL-TV. Here, a brief ray of hope came when Guy looked me squarely in the eye and asked me a question in which lurked a hint of salvation. "Do you drink?" he demanded. "Like a fish!" I shot back, trembling with fear that the answer might leave some doubt.

"Let's go," he announced, rather than rejoined. He then led me, at a half run, to a door that led to Rampart Street and a half block along that fabled pathway to an establishment called Johnnie's.

It was while working for WWL-TV that I met a Jesuit priest. Father Aloysius Benedict Goodspeed. The Jesuits owned WWL-TV and Loyola University, and Father Goodspeed was treasurer of both. Thus he held the pursestrings. He also liked to spend long lunches at Brennan's Restaurant in the French Quarter. I often was appointed to go with the good Father, and I came to love and admire him. I had studied the Bible and we would discuss that great book, and the philosophy therein. Being argumentative by nature (except when being given a job), I would dispute with him, test his arguments, and sometimes barely make it back to the studio to do my news broadcast. And I learned.

I learned that I did not believe all the things I thought I believed, and that he didn't either. We had great fun. And later he sincerely regretted my leaving WWL-TV to go to KMOX-TV in St. Louis. But what could I do? They insisted!

Owned as it was, by the CBS network, KMOX-TV could hardly be blamed for putting me into an arena where I would be called to New York. I did not resist. I couldn't. After all, there was that deal between Betty Jo and God and since she had failed to call it off, and He had gotten busy with other pursuits, the whole thing was still in effect. I didn't go to the network, I went to WCBS-TV, the flagship station.

At WCBS-TV I was put in charge of those news stories falling within my special sphere of interest, that is auto mechanics, archeology, and pool hustling. They did not make me an anchorman as I had been at New Orleans and St. Louis. I did not qualify. In New York an anchorman is a person who has a deep voice, lots of neatly styled hair, and doesn't wear glasses. I guess it was my glasses.

My best, that's what I gave to WCBS-TV, and I've never figured out exactly what went wrong. As a street reporter I accepted and reported on assignments from one end of the city to another. One I particularly remember was the discovery, by the pertinent authorities, of a whiskey still in Brooklyn. There, in an old tenement building, someone had set up a distillery for the production of whiskey, corn whiskey. There were vats and vats of corn mash, a huge boiling kettle, pipes running everywhere, and numerous gallons of the finished product stored nearby. The whole affair had been discovered when a floor gave way, and the resulting noise attracted attention.

My report could possibly have disappointed some of the elder and wiser journalists at WCBS, but I don't understand quite why. I noted that the piping and tubing should have been copper rather than iron. The underpinning of the collapsed vat was shoddy, or it wouldn't have collapsed; the special venom of my report centered, however, on the product itself. It was awful. Badly cooked, badly bottled, not aged in charred kegs as it should be, and lacking that, not even tinted a bit with iodine so it would at least have the proper color. Clearly the work of amateurs, and hardly worthy of my notice at all. I did point out that the amateurism of the distillers was approached only by that of the authorities who failed to discover the still for what obviously was a period of several years while it corroded its way through a floor, in spite of the fact that this still had an aroma that could be detected for at least a mile in any downwind direction. My editors felt I had missed the point. Fortunately, I was soon required by ABC. Betty Jo and God were still at work.

Ah, ABC. That was over a decade ago. I guess nobody else wanted me during that time. Tempted often to give it up, I always stayed aboard for lack of a safe haven elsewhere. This, after all, was a network job.

Since it was obvious that I was destined to spend my life in broadcasting, I had developed over the years a desire, or rather a compulsion, to be a correspondent. Correspondents, you see, are reporters who get to travel everywhere, and stick their noses into all sorts of things, and get paid for it. Harry Reasoner once said that he believed people who became correspondents were actually those who wanted to be "everything," realized they couldn't, so found it necessary to take up an occupation that would put them in touch with the people who *do* "everything."

That's as good a job description for a correspondent as I ever heard.

CBS didn't want me to be a correspondent, but ABC did. Word had gotten to Av Westin, then executive producer of the "ABC Evening News with Howard K. Smith," that this fellow Kincaid would be willing to go to Viet Nam. In those days, people were not exactly lining up to take numbers for the chance to go to Viet Nam. Westin was an old CBS hand, and the fact that I had spent seven years in those hallowed halls worked in my favor; so I was once again hired without having asked for the job.

The way it worked, I was coming to the end of my contract with CBS, and an agent called and said he had one from ABC, and would I please come over and sign it. Several years later a functionary in the ABC personnel office discovered that I had never filed an application, and he contacted me to see how that had happened.

By this time I already suspected God and Betty Jo, but even though I explained it all he failed to see the logic of it. He insisted that I fill out an application, but I told him I'd feel silly applying for a job I'd already had for years. I never saw him again. I think he got a government job.

ABC gave me a short orientation period in New York to prepare me for the assignment to Viet Nam. A few local assignments, a trip to Washington to be briefed by the Pentagon and State Department, and I was off.

I don't know if I will ever completely sort out the next chapter of my life. It stands totally apart from all my other experiences. Traveling and reporting Viet Nam, I saw land reform programs that worked, pacification programs that didn't, battles that were won, and more that were lost, and an abundance of misery.

Part of me can rationalize that my country was mistakenly involved in a civil conflict between two factions that wanted to control another country...their country...and that the whole thing was none of our business. But, another part of me feels we had an obligation to help in the establishment of a free country in South Viet Nam.

Of course, South Viet Nam was not a perfect democracy; neither is ours. But they had an excuse: they'd never had any practice. I've been away from Viet Nam for more than a decade now, but it's still too fresh in my memory. There's still a lot of pain—mainly mental, partly physical from an injury I sustained there. But I must admit to some guilt feelings, too, though I'm not sure I feel guilt about the same things others do. Maybe, with the passage of another decade or so, I'll be able to sort it out.

About six months before I was scheduled to leave Viet Nam I was injured. Some divine providence has created a mental block which erased much of the experience of a helicopter crash from my memory. The parts I can remember are bad enough, and have no place in what I hope will be a happy book.

At any rate, I required about six months of repair and recovery, and I was lucky enough to be able to spend it in Hong Kong. Lucky because Hong Kong was the city of choice for a very talented British spinal surgeon named A. R. Hodgson. Professor Hodgson (among the British, professors outrank doctors) and a team of his associates went hunting around among my undamaged parts and found some pieces of rib and thigh that did very nicely to rebuild a severely damaged backbone. The result was that I was spared the partial paralysis earlier medical opinion had decreed almost a certainty. I don't have to tell you how grateful I was.

ABC paid the bills, and employed me during the recovery period as a "China Watcher." A "China Watcher" is a person who lives in Hong Kong, works for an American network or newspaper, and has the time and patience to wade through the rhetoric on the English language service of the official newswires from Peking.

It's a job that takes time, or did in those days. The Chinese were not terribly complimentary, but Chinese is a language with a relatively small number of usable insults. So the Official News Agency of the People's Democratic Republic of China (HSINHUA) had to use the same insults over and over.

A typical dispatch from Peking would open: "The imperialist lackeys of Wall Street and their running dogs...." You'd have to wade through several lines of this to learn that they were talking about the American military forces in Vietnam. The next story would be about an American trade delegation to Japan which would invariably be described as a group of imperialist lackeys of Wall Street and their running dogs... a group of nuns operating an orphanage in Thailand... same thing. You got the idea the writers up there in Peking didn't think highly of imperialism, Wall Street, or running dogs.

China-watching for me was reading miles of this garbage every day, and boiling it down to five or six usable paragraphs to transmit back to New York for ABC Radio. The Bureau chief for ABC in Hong Kong in those days was Ted Koppel, lately of "Nightline," and one of the most talented journalists this country has ever produced. Ted wasn't famous when we became friends, and neither was I, but we had some fun, and I had the chance to probe the mind that makes "Nightline" the only really new approach to news now available on network television.

On top of all that, Ted sustained me during a difficult time when about half of the news executives at ABC in New York thought I was too sick to be of any further use, and the other half thought I was too lazy. They were probably both right. But Ted got me to work, and convinced me that I could work, and that it would ultimately be worth it.

When the time came for me to be returned to the real world, there was a great debate in the halls of ABC News Executivedom about where I should be assigned. And since Professor Hodgson recommended that I be in a warm climate, and the month was January, I was assigned to Chicago.

Ah, Chicago... I arrived on a day when the temperature was six below zero and a teacher's strike was starting, which had to be covered on the picket lines of course. And I don't remember being warm again for four years. Chicago, in the early seventies, was the ABC bureau that covered everything that was happening any place in the country that was not New York, Washington, or Los Angeles. You could get anywhere from O'Hare Airport.

I won't bore you with details of the many trips I made from there, and the stories I covered, but it developed that ABC felt I was particularly suited to "one of a kind" stories. If the Census Bureau determined the exact center of the nation, population-wise, I would draw the assignment. (In 1970, it was in the middle of Lawrence Friederich's cornfield about four miles from Mascoutah, Illinois.) When there was a disaster in West Virginia, I became the Appalachian disaster specialist. ABC discovered that I had grown up on a farm, so I got to be ABC's agricultural reporter. I even did some sports stories, and a story about women who made quilts, and a story about a town that raised all sorts of cain when a factory whistle they'd been waking up to for eighty years was shut down. And a story about...but I said I wouldn't bore you with all that.

I never could be trusted.

Finally, ABC moved me to Washington where some of the executives thought I could be trained to behave as a good correspondent should. Somehow, I guess I disappointed them. I could never get it through my head that a trivial event in Washington was more important than a major event in some other part of the country or the world.

When I wasn't on the road chasing down a farmer, or a coal mine disaster, the bureau would send me up to Capitol Hill, or over to the White House, to relieve one of the real correspondents while he went to lunch, or to get a haircut. (ABC also thought I didn't take haircuts quite seriously enough.)

It was my habit not to report anything if I did not consider it important, and thus I missed some rare items of earthshaking importance—such as the time the House of Representatives gave Pete Rose a standing ovation. Things like that. I can see in retrospect why ABC had its doubts about me.

Back last Thanksgiving some turkey growers showed up at the White House and gave President Reagan a turkey. Luckily, I was not ABC's man at the White House that day. I probably would have stayed in the pressroom and played solitaire while that momentous scene was being played out in the Rose Garden. I saw it on television, and realized that the weight of it would have been lost on me until too late. But, as fortune would have it, Sam Donaldson was there, and the moment was preserved for history.

Seriously, I know Sam, and respect him, and I believe he was as embarrassed at reporting such a spectacle as the President of the United States trying to calm a live turkey in the presence of a news corps that represented the eyes and ears of the world.

But Sam was probably not as embarrassed as the turkey, who given the choice, probably would not have attended the ceremony in the first place. Sam, and many of his colleagues, have lived in Washington too long. I am certain of it. I have no further information on the turkey.

There came a time when I realized that I would never fully accept, or be accepted by, the network journalism fraternity. Further, I was tired of living most of my life on airplanes, in hotels and motels, searching for a story better than the last one.

So, there was only one obvious course of action. I had to leave ABC and buy a farm.

You may notice that I've neglected so far to mention home and family. Being a correspondent doesn't leave much time for such frivolities, but many correspondents have them anyway. I know some who have had two or three (not at the same time, of course).

However, as luck would have it, I have a wife and a daughter and a fervent love for both of them. So they played a role in the evolution of my thinking. Simply, I wanted a lifestyle that would allow me to be with them for at least a part of every day, and not just on occasional weekends when ABC had nothing better for me to do.

The next problem was how to divorce ABC. I was still under a contract, and since I had been raised to honor contracts, no matter what, my problem was to get ABC to call off the deal.

It was desperation that drove me one day to sit down at my desk in Washington and compose a memo. Network folks set great store by memos. They send each other thousands of them. They write memos to confirm recent phone conversations. They write memos to revise earlier memos. Memos are to network executives what eucalyptus leaves are to a koala bear. Memos are the currency of executive commerce.

My memo was simple, and oh so effective. It said, "I will no longer accept any assignment that adversely affects my moral, mental, or physical health." And I signed it.

HERESY! That was the only word to describe the attitude of ABC management. When questioned, I explained that I would continue to do my job, and do it as professionally as possible, but, *if* I determined that my health, mental, moral, or physical was in jeopardy, I would pull back, and wait until conditions improve. Any coal miner, or plumber, or history professor would do the same, and be perfectly within his rights, and if someone tried to deny him those rights, you'd send me out to tell his story.

"You don't understand Kincaid," they responded, "we can't have correspondents going around deciding what's in their own best interest." They didn't say it quite like that, but the message was clear.

A few hours later my agent informed me that I'd better find somebody very powerful and apologize, or I'd be fired. I didn't tell him that I figured my severance pay would just about make the down payment on a farm.

When my wife, my daughter, my father-in-law and I drove to Prince Edward County, Virginia to look at a farm at a place called Elam, we hadn't an inkling of how it would change our lives. We had seen the ad in a catalogue from the Atkins Realty Company in Farmville. The ad said, "Buy a piece of History."

We hadn't made the trip from Washington just to look at the Elam farm. We had, in fact, picked several that looked promising, and a very patient real estate agent named Bill Benhoff helped us cover the territory.

"Whipporwill" farm was too finished. The house was new and efficient and might have fit very well into a suburb. There were others more or less the same, but when we rounded a bend in a gravel road, and looked down into a shallow valley at Elam... we knew we were home.

It took several more months to wind up affairs in Washington, buy the farm from Louise Foreman, heir to the last Elams to live in the old house, and finally move into our two-hundred-year-old treasure. On the day we moved in, the moving crew that had taken our worldly goods out of a very modern house in Silver Spring, Maryland, asked, not once but several times, if we were sure this was the right address.

The house at Elam is, at least in part, more than two hundred years old. Originally, it was a double log cabin. Overhead, there's a hand-crimped tin roof, the kind that leaks here and there, but is a joy to sleep under on a summer night when there's a soft rain falling.

It needed all sorts of work, and we set about it with high hopes and willing hands, and fully expect to complete, at least

the preliminary restoration, sometime during the current century. The detail work may need a little longer.
The next order of business was to find a job within a few hours drive of Elam. There was no big hurry. We had a small cash cushion. And by this time I had figured out Betty Jo's arrangement with the Almighty, and knew that I would be drafted again in no time.
No time figured out to be almost a year.
The cash cushion dwindled and my wife and I took some odd jobs here and there to replenish it, grew an enormous garden, and sold some cars for a Farmville dealer named "Moon" Mullins. Honest. And had just about decided that the Betty Jo factor had ceased to operate when I met a Virginia Senator named Hunter Andrews.
Longwood College in Farmville was hosting a debate among several Democrats who wanted to be Virginia's next United States Senator. I was asked to moderate the debate, and I accepted, and I guess I did a pretty good job. It wasn't easy to keep four Democrats quiet while a fifth Democrat had his say, but I did it. All got about the same amount of time, and no blood was shed.
That was no small accomplishment. Democrats are generally nice to each other except when they want the same job. When that happens, stand back! Give me a cageful of tigers anytime...you can reason with tigers. With Democrats, nothing short of naked force will do.
I guess Senator Andrews was impressed with me, because he came up to me at a cocktail party the Longwood folks gave for the survivors of the debate. We talked for a few minutes and he developed the information that I was currently "at liberty," and would more than likely be there for awhile. Then he told me, with a certainty only to be found in a particular few, "I know a man who needs you. He doesn't know it yet, but he needs you, and you need him."
That's how I came to meet Tom Chisman, then the owner of WVEC-TV.
It took some time, but Tom and I finally agreed that I would come to Tidewater and anchor Channel 13's two major newscasts. Our negotiations ended in a handshake.
There are still people around who consider a handshake the most solid contract of all. I do. If you shake the hand of a person of honor. My handshake with Tom Chisman has been in force for nearly four years now, and, God willing, has many

years to run.

Before I made my first broadcast, I asked Tom if it would be all right if I entered a little personal "note" from time to time. He allowed that a person with the mileage I had on me should have such a right. "Go ahead," he said, "I'll let you know if you step too far." I haven't heard anything from him since on the subject but encouragement.

And that's how these "Notes" came to be.

You can see that it's all Betty Jo's fault.

CHAPTER 1

The farm country I grew up in down Arkansas way was remote enough to avoid being overburdened with modern conveniences.

Most of the conveniences, in fact, didn't reach there till well after World War II.

Indoor plumbing, air conditioning, telephones that work and such are all necessities these days, but I can remember when we got along quite well without them.

I wouldn't exactly care to go back, but I dearly enjoy....

LOOKING BACK

November 30, 1979.

As any parent knows, the satisfaction that children derive from toys is directly proportional to the amount of noise that toy will make just at a time when the parent is deeply involved in some activity that calls for quiet.

What with computer technology children are now able to inflict greater strains on parents' nerves than ever before. If they're not affected by the clippity-clop of a horse, you can hit'em with the sound of an alien starship being destroyed.

But I'm old enough to remember simpler times. We didn't have the technology when I was a child, but we had the will and the creativeness.

And sometimes I wonder if modern children ever know the pure pleasure of building a tower of wooden blocks, Lincoln Logs, Tinker Toy parts, and boxes, six feet high or so. And then, quietly and deliberately, taking away just the bottom block.

Performed on a wooden floor it was guaranteed to bring any mom out of the kitchen at a dead run.

She'd be too relieved to find you alive to punish you severely. And if you had to go to bed early, at least you went with a sense of achievement.

January 23, 1980.

They had "Jack" stories in the Ozark Mountains where I grew up, too. And like the Jack the Ferrum College students talk about, the central character was one who made his way in life by his wits.

25

Our neighborhood storyteller once described the sort of fellow he had in mind when he told his Jack tales.

Said, he ain't exactly honest and he ain't exactly dishonest....

...he's smart, but he only acts smart when absolutely necessary....

...he's reasonably nice, if it don't require too much physical effort....

...he's the sort of feller that's bound to wind up in jail...or maybe Congress.

June 6, 1980.

When I was a youth, the word vacation had quite another meaning.

The main meaning, as I remember, was that we didn't have to go to school. And I could never understand why my mother wasn't as excited at that prospect as I.

The secondary, but almost as important meaning was that the weather for going barefooted had arrived.

My mother never really appreciated that aspect of vacation time either, but I suppose it was because she spent a lot of her summer digging out splinters and treating stone bruises.

Going someplace expensive was a question that never came up. Farms with crops and gardens and animals don't take kindly to being abandoned.

It wasn't terribly glamorous, I guess, but we didn't know any better and you sure couldn't beat the price.

July 16, 1980.

In my youth down in Arkansas we had heat such as today's in Tidewater on a regular basis, and I suspect it wasn't all that rare here and in other parts of the country.

We had two principal means of air conditioning in those times. One was a paper fan with a religious picture on one side, a funeral home advertisement on the other, and a sort of a large popsicle stick stapled on for a handle.

The other was watermelon.

Our parents either raised them or bought them from a neighbor. But us boys acquired our watermelons by art, and cooled them in the creek.

We didn't steal other things . . . that would have been dishonest.

But if you ever tasted a snitched watermelon, cooled in a spring-fed creek, and eaten by hand in the company of your partners in crime, you know the taste of nature's rarest prize.

July 21, 1980.
When I was a youngster I believed that if I ever could grow to be as tall as my mother, that I could then consider myself an adult.

Sometime after the age of ten, I discovered that almost everyone in North America was taller than my mother, but I never stopped looking up to her.

The reason I mention this is that she's visiting with me here in Tidewater, decided to come out from Texas and enjoy our cool weather.

I've been bragging about Tidewater all along, the people especially, and my mother has always insisted that I associate with nice people.

So, behave yourselves, or I'll be in all sorts of trouble.

May 8, 1981.
What with Mother's Day coming up, I got to thinking about my mother this afternoon, and what a remarkable job she did with some pretty questionable prospects.

When World War II broke out, my elder brothers and my father were eligible to participate, and they did; and my mother was left with me and a forty-acre farm in Arkansas.

I don't know which required the most raising, me or the farm. But she took the job at a time when Doctor Spock hadn't even written his first book. So, naturally she didn't know the first thing about rearing a kid.

She said "No" a lot, and I knew at the time that that was a mistake, and told her so. But she didn't listen. She also sent me out to cut a switch from time to time, and then used the switch to reinforce some of the arbitrary decisions she made with which I had failed to comply.

But, in spite of all that repression I stayed mostly in school and mostly out of jail and survived to adulthood.

I guess it was luck.

Curiously enough, I don't even hold it against her.

I guess it was the sugar cookies.

I remember the "Nos" and the long dreadful trip to cut a switch.

But I remember those sugar cookies even better.

27

June 1, 1981.

As a youngster in Arkansas, growing up in the country, I learned early on that it was best to leave wild animals alone in the wild.

My elders advised me that it was never a good practice to pick up any sort of wild creature, no matter how helpless and cuddly it might look. Like most boys, however, it took a few object lessons before I was totally convinced.

I tried once to free a full-grown raccoon from a trap; but the raccoon obviously gave me points for being of the same breed that had set the trap in the first place, and no points at all for compassion. I wound up with more tooth marks than a well-buttered ear of sweet corn.

Luckily, I didn't manage to set him free before the town doctor got a chance to observe him and be sure he wasn't rabid.

Another time I investigated an animal I had only glimpsed running into a thicket of honeysuckle.—Just about the time I waded far enough into the honeysuckle to spot my quarry, he let go with his defense mechanism, and I learned that the animal I had spotted was a skunk.

I had gotten close enough that no one within fifty feet of me could possibly disbelieve that I had indeed found a skunk, and a powerfully talented one at that.

My mother let me sleep outside for a few days...downwind.

July 9, 1981.

I had the good fortune as a child to live in a house where money was too short to be spent on trashy literature, comic books and such. But the classics were there.

I didn't think it was such an honor at the time, but I was encouraged to read a lot; and Shakespeare was among the things I was encouraged to read.

It seemed, even then, that a lot of the lines he wrote fit into a modern context.

I went looking for some of them this afternoon.

The first I found was from Henry VI:

"Now tis the spring...and the weeds are shallow rooted

Suffer them now...and they'll o'ergrow the garden."

My garden at Elam is living proof of the accuracy of that

statement.

In *Love's Labors Lost,* Shakespeare has a moth say: "They have been at a great feast of languages and they have stolen the scraps...."

If you've ever been to a political convention you know precisely what Old Will had in mind.

Elsewhere he tells us that not even a philosopher can bear a toothache patiently. Yessir, Shakespeare was a perceptive man, no doubt of it. Maybe even a prophet.

He foresaw the modern lawmaking process in *Much Ado About Nothing:*

"O what men dare do, he said, what men may do, what men daily do, not knowing what they do...."

August 24, 1981.

Those of us who are old enough to remember a comedian named Herb Shriner will know, of course, that the air guitar is not the most fantastic instrument ever devised.

That would have to be the fenorton.

For those of you too young to remember Herb Shriner, I'll have to tell you about it, because the last great fenortonist was a personal friend of Herb's.

The fenorton, of course, was a wind instrument, twenty-seven feet long, which was played by blowing into both ends at the same time.

As I'm sure you can appreciate, you had to be fast to be a fenortonist, and careful too.

The finest fenortonist I ever knew was Sedgewick Stockley, who met a sad end one day when he was running from one end of his fenorton to the other, trying for a high "C."

Old Sedge slipped on some sand that had been left there by a soft-shoe dancer and fell through the harp. They didn't figure they could operate on him, so they tried laminating him, and it worked. Except that old Sedge wound up with a split personality.

He thought he was the University of Arkansas marching band.

I gave up the fenorton along about then and took up playing a comb, but I finally gave that up, too.

A comb just doesn't sound right without a good fenorton background.

29

September 11, 1981.

I read an interesting article today on the plight of today's college students. According to the article, higher costs of education are getting together with smaller amounts of federal aid and making it harder for all the people who want to go to college.

It got me to remembering.

When my older brothers came back from World War II, they—and a lot like them—wanted to go to college.

And they did, with the help of the GI Bill and working wives, and full-time jobs of their own, and part-time jobs on weekends. It took some extra years, but they finally got college degrees, and so did their wives, and they even paid off some loans they made.

Of course, in those days when you borrowed money, you borrowed it from a bank, and were expected to pay it back...on time...with interest.

Anyway, this article I was reading today said things have gotten so bad that a lot of students can't make it without getting jobs or borrowing money.

Sorta the way it was thirty-five years ago, only then nobody seemed to think that was anything to get terribly upset about.

CHAPTER 2

I never got around to going to college, so it isn't surprising that I never took any courses in Economics.

I'm not even sure if you're supposed to capitalize it—or them.

I have had a number of years of practical experience in the field, learning by trial and error. Mostly error.

When I see how often the experts are right or wrong, I feel downright brilliant. Therefore, I muddle along with a personal theory that works just about as often as it doesn't. Sorta like the experts. I call it....

AN INNOCENT ABROAD IN THE ECONOMY

March 29, 1979.

An obvious solution to the high price and short supply of gasoline is all around us, and largely being ignored.

Potholes.

When was the last time you drove along a street filled with potholes at speeds above the limit?

It's well known that cars burn much less gas at lower speeds, and cars with broken axles and blown out tires use even less.

Potholes would also lower the unemployment figures in the auto repair and tire industries.

Potholes are an unappreciated blessing that we get absolutely free and can always be sure of having in plentiful numbers, if only we use them properly.

December 13, 1979.

Some poet once observed, very truly I think, that an open fire warms the soul as well as the body.

And, that we see that such a fire can come about as the happy accident of problem solving, seems to make it just that much more worthwhile.

Perhaps that is the strength of our people, that we employ our ingenuity to turn problems into profit. Happily, it happens all the time.

Gasoline was once a waste by-product of the refining process that we had to find some way to get rid of. See how well we did that?

Today, the rumors started that the oil-producing nations are about to raise their prices again, and that's a problem for us.

But oil is a finite resource, and that's a problem for them. Whether our problem will be greater than theirs may be open to question.

But, looking at the record, I'd have to bet on us. So far, American ingenuity has all the appearance of being in limitless supply.

March 10, 1980.

I suppose it shouldn't surprise us, or even anger us, that taxes, like everything else, seem to be getting higher all the time.

But, after all, President Carter did tell us a while back that we have to get used to paying more, and getting less.

I've decided to follow the advice I saw once on a calendar. You know, under a thought for the day, or something like that.

The advice was simple: We should all strive to be happy and live within our means.

Even if we have to borrow the money to do it.

April 15, 1980.

In that I have never had enough money all at one time to invest in stocks, or bonds, or commodities, and so forth, I have largely ignored the science of economics.

I've listened to economists, and read their statements, and failed a hundred percent of the time to understand a bit of it. However, I ran across a piece of economic advice today that I understand, and that bears repeating.

The source: Billy Rose, who was married innumerable times and thus must have been an expert on economics.

The advice: never invest in anything that eats or needs repainting.

April 29, 1980.

It's interesting to note that all those banks, the ones that for many weeks were in the news every few days raising the prime rate, are now lowering the prime rate.

That doesn't mean they don't want as much for the use of their money; they just can't get as much.

The reasoning is, it seems, that 18% of something is better than 20% of nothing.

I believe it may be a result of an old inflation-fighting technique used by many Americans for years—one that works pretty well. It consists of learning a key phrase, and repeating it over and over again when the opportunity presents itself.

It's a simple phrase that goes like this: "That's too much, I'd better wait."

Does it work? Well, take a look at Detroit's cars lately.

We may be seeing the start of something small.

May 6, 1980.

Last week I repeated a formula for inflation fighting consisting of learning a simple phrase, and repeating it over and over again while shopping.

Something like, "That's too much for that, I think I'll get along without it for now . . . ."

Well, since that time I've received a number of letters and phone calls from other harried consumers who have inflation-fighting phrases of their own. I thought it might be nice to pass a few along.

How about, "I think I'll tune this one up and drive it a while?"

Or, "Perhaps you have a model in stock that isn't gold plated?"

Or—and this one was my favorite: "If I could afford to spend that kind of money I wouldn't be seen in a place like this."

June 4, 1980.

With prices as high as they are for raw materials, some major industries are turning to the government—read taxpayer—for help.

Take butter cookies for example.

Danish butter cookies are undercutting American butter cookies right here in the American market.

Now that might not bother you, but it bothers the Deer Park Baking Company of Hammonton, New Jersey.

It's a conspiracy.

The European Economic Community holds the prices of eggs, sugar, butter, and flour artificially low, and the result is that the Danish butter cookie cartel can flood the American market with butter cookies that are not superior to but cheaper than American butter cookies.

So, hand in hand with the Commerce Department, the American butter cookie interests went to the International Trade Commission, seeking admission to Uncle Sam's cookie jar.

After all, it's the American way.

But, the ITC turned them down—said, in effect, and I'm sure you've been expecting this: Sorry, but that's the way the cookie crumbles.

July 9, 1980.

I was talking the other day with a friend of mine from West Virginia who happens also to be a Justice of that state's Supreme Court.

Kincaid, sez he, I've got the solution to this slump the automobile industry is in.

Judge, sez I, I think you just dangled a participle, but go ahead.

He sez, what if the government took all that money that it's about to give the car companies, and gave it instead to those poor unfortunate Americans who now own big gas guzzling cars, and can't afford to buy small fuel efficient cars...you know...the poor and middle class...and give it to them in the form of low-interest loans for the specific purpose of buying American-made small fuel-efficient cars.

That way, sez he, the auto industry would get a shot in the arm and the government would get its money back.

I figured, sez I, that there was some catch to it.

September 8, 1980.

I saw reports all day about this, that, and the other thing that's going up in price.

Ford's new smaller cars will be smaller, according to a wire report, in everything but price. Chrysler's K cars make the same promise, and so on. Milk—get ready to pay another two cents a gallon soon, and watch the price rise in the months to come. Meat—what can I tell you that you don't already know!

Produce—mainly because of the dry weather—is going up. The weather will also account for higher prices in just about everything else we eat.

Clothing—well, it's the same old story.

So, how about a bit of good news, a ray of hope, a holding of the line?

Here goes: The Leaf Confectionary Company recently announced that it will, despite the price of sugar, continue to sell penny gumballs for a penny.

There now, don't you feel better?

November 14, 1980.

If Joe Foulkes is right, and he usually is, we can expect our weather to start downhill in coming days, and the heating season will be upon us.

It raises questions as to how the wood cartel is doing.

I mentioned my suspicions last fall that there will be a wood cartel now that we heat our farmhouse at Elam with wood; and while I still can't prove anything, I'm just as sure as Christmas that there's a wood cartel.

I base my suspicions on what is now, to my mind, an immutable law of nature, one that has proven valid over and over again.

It works like this: Anything I want or need just one of goes down in price only after I have bought one.

Anything I want or need on a continuing basis goes up in price steadily so long as the want or need continues.

If you don't believe me, price a cord of wood.

December 3, 1980.

I don't mind telling you, I'm worried about this peanut shortage, the fact that there will only be about half as many peanuts this year as the peanut industry needs to meet demand.

However, I'd like to speak out against this idea of importing foreign peanuts to make up for the shortfall.

Some people just don't pay attention. That's the very way we got into the oil mess we're in.

It got too costly to produce domestic oil, then there wasn't enough, and before you know it, embargo, price rises, and cartels all over the place.

I predict that peanut importation will lead to the establishment of an organization of peanut-producing countries.

Dependence on the foreign peanut could lead to the spectre of price spirals in peanut butter, crackerjacks, and the domestic Baby Ruth candy bar.

Write your congressman now—before it's too late.

May 12, 1981.

Since Sunday was Mother's Day, I completely overlooked the fact that it was also Tax Freedom Day.

Tax Freedom Day, as you'll remember, is that day of the year when the average American breadwinner theoretically has won enough bread to pay the Government what it requires to keep body and soul together, and then is—again this is theory—then is privileged to start winning some bread and keeping said bread.

Of course, this is all just theory, since we pay the government all year round, average or not, and besides, Americans are very rarely average.

But it got me to thinking? Wouldn't it be nice if we had a tax holiday?

A week or a month sometime during the year when we could collect everything we make, without deductions, and let government take a larger bite during the other weeks or months to make up for it.

Seeing the difference, of course, might make us wonder what government does with all that money, which is ours after all, even when they get it before we do.

We might even get a proprietary feeling about our money, like maybe it could be used to better advantage, or more efficiently.

It's just a thought, and probably a silly one at that.

But I wonder about it anyway.

July 13, 1981.

Those figures from the Tax Foundation are a little discouraging.

They show that the median family in America—which is according to them, a family with one wage earner and two children and, I presume, one other adult—the median family saw its income rise by 130 percent in the last ten years.

That's good, right?

Not so good; in that same ten years the income tax bite on that same family has increased 200 percent and the Social Security taxes have gone up 300 percent.

The way it works out, according to the Tax Foundation, this median family wound up losing 5 percent of its buying power in that ten-year period.

I'm sure the folks who whipped up these statistics mean well, but I still have trouble relating to them.

What I need is a table that breaks down the financial condition of a fellow that has a wife and a daughter, and an apartment, and a two hundred-year-old farm with plumbing that freezes, and four dogs, and an undetermined number of cats, and chickens that only occasionally lay eggs, and a yardful of ducks that can't be eaten because they all have names.

I take median to mean sorta in the middle.

Well sir, just how in the middle can you get?

July 15, 1981.

I don't pretend to understand global economics. But I do have a rudimentary grasp of the law of supply and demand. Under that law, I've always been told, those things that are desirable and in short supply will cost more, and vice versa.

Now here's my current problem. And I'm sure there's a reasonable explanation. The oil companies are paying more to the Arabs than ever before for crude oil. Well, when raw materials cost more, the profit margin goes down. Right? Wrong. The quarterly earnings are better than ever.

I'm also told that there's a surplus of gasoline right now. The price goes down. Right? Wrong.

It all leads me to believe that we, the consuming public, are getting an overabundance of the vice—and none of the versa.

August 5, 1981.

Now that the Reagan Administration's new tax cut is a matter of law, we'll be seeing all sorts of charts and graphs purporting to tell us what it means to us.

You know the sort of thing I mean...the average family of four with two incomes, the family with all those qualities that the statisticians trot out, and whose circumstances never seem to apply to us at all.

I've got a simpler method of calculating the impact of the tax cut.

Take your last paycheck and get your wife, or somebody who knows how to use one of those little electronic calculators, and get him or her to figure out what five percent of the money Uncle kept out would come to; that's how much more you'll get to keep in October.

If you're the average television anchorman, your wife, or someone you know who knows how to operate one of those little electronic calculators, will tell you that it's hardly enough to buy batteries for one of those little electronic calculators.

However, you may want to know anyway...if for no other reason than to comfort yourself with the knowledge that you'll get that extra money all the way into January... when the Social Security taxes go up.

That's Thirteen News and a note of despair.

September 8, 1981.

I heard this morning that there's a coffee glut—too many coffee beans.

Well, I drink a lot of coffee, so I immediately latched onto this piece of news as good news...thinking that the law of supply and demand would take hold and the price of coffee would come down.

I thought that up until I met with this economist friend of mine who also drinks a lot of coffee. Nossir, he said, this coffee glut will work economically the same way the oil glut works.

When there's too much coffee around, the price has to go up, because people won't buy enough of it to satisfy the greed of the coffee-producing nations which see an opportunity to turn some pretty handsome windfall profits.

I see, I said, so to get the price of coffee down we have to drink less.

No, that wouldn't work either, since those who sell coffee would have to raise prices to compensate for the fact that people are using less, sort of like electricity, and natural gas.

So, sez I, if there's too much coffee the price goes up; if we cut back on consumption, the price goes up; and if there's a shortage the price goes up.

Right, says the economist, it's the new law of supply and demand.

Those who have the supply get to make the demands.

September 9, 1981.

I'll be the first to admit that I don't understand economics. But, it does fall my lot each afternoon to prepare the stock market report.

You know, the Dow Jones Average did so and so, closing at so and so.

I get the figures from the Associated Press wire, and since I don't understand the stock market, I usually go along

with what the Associated Press analyst says.
 Yesterday, I reported that concern over high interest rates caused another decline in stock prices, and a local investor called and said that wasn't the case at all. He said it's all due to internal market pressures, with buyers adding liquidity to their portfolios, waiting to buy when the next surge comes.
 Boy, was my face red. I hadn't considered that at all.
 Then I read another economist today who said that the consumer confidence index is down and that the trend is indecisive.
 Sonofagun....
 So, armed with this knowledge I spent an hour or so with my Webster's and my thesaurus and a copy of the *Farmer's Almanac* and came up with a translation.
 It goes like this: Folks with money don't know much more about where the economy is going than folks without money, so they figure to try to hold onto it until they do.

September 16, 1981.
 I don't know about you, but I'm beginning to feel a little over-experted.
 Every time you turn on a television set these days, or pick up a newspaper, there's another expert telling us just exactly what's about to happen, and why.
 Then, just when we figure we know, there's another expert telling us that just the opposite is about to happen, and why. The problem I have is with the whys.
 They always sound perfectly reasonable.
 I always listen or read very carefully, at least I try to, and the arguments for a certain scenario make perfect sense. Then, another expert comes along and convinces me that the first expert was utterly and completely wrong, and that argument makes sense.
 Take the economic situation for example.
 I read an expert in the *Wall Street Journal* who says Wall Street is shaky because the President's budget-cutting program isn't fully in effect just yet.
 Another says it's because the program doesn't go far enough.
 And a third says it's because it goes too far.
 Personally, I think it's because they don't know which experts to believe any more than I do.

39

CHAPTER 3

Back during the primaries that led up to the Carter-Ford campaigns of '76, ABC assigned me to follow the fortunes of one of the Democrats who wanted the job.

I did not care for the snows of New Hampshire, but I liked Fred Harris. Fred is a former senator from Oklahoma whose ideas got him branded as a populist. And I guess he is one.

When all the other candidates were hopping around in Lear jets and private planes, Fred, with me and Jed DuVal of CBS, was traveling in a rented motor home, borrowing money for tolls, gasoline, and Big Macs.

His battle cry still rings in my ears when I see evidence that government is wasting our time, money, or national honor.

Quoth Fred:

"THEY OUGHT NOT TO BE DOING THAT"

October 31, 1979.

I noted with interest an item on the Associated Press wire today.

It was to the effect that Speaker of the House Tip O'Neill had announced that the House should complete its business today by six-thirty since some of the members had expressed an interest in going out to trick or treat.

It occurs to me that Speaker O'Neill was joking.

But it also occurs that they might be pretty good at it....

...what with all the practice they get.

November 1, 1979.

Though they squabble about things like taxes, and federal funding, and foreign treaties, the House and Senate have come up with something they can agree on.

Will Rogers. They've agreed, the House and Senate have, to honor the memory of the great humorist on the occasion of what would have been his hundredth birthday November 4th.

Will Rogers would probably be pleased. After all, it was the Congress that provided a great deal of his material.

I doubt, though, that the honor would change Will Rogers' opinion of politics which he defined as "applesauce."

Rogers maintained, in fact, that he didn't write jokes; he just watched Congress and reported the facts.

November 2, 1979.
Did your congressman send you a calendar last year? If not, that may mean you fall outside of a circle of twenty-five hundred close friends and favored constituents.

The way it works...each year, the government prints up a million dollars or so worth of calendars; using our money of course; gives twenty-five hundred to each congressman and five hundred to each senator; and, again using our money for mailing and manpower, ships them out to us.

The House passed a bill last year to stop this practice, but that was after last year's calendars had been printed and mailed.

The bill didn't apply to this year and the calendars are being printed up again. Your chance and mine of getting one—about two hundred fifty to one.

On second thought, my chances are probably zero.

November 15, 1979.
Life is certainly full of contradictions.

We live in a country where the government uses our tax dollars to encourage people to stop smoking and other tax dollars to subsidize farmers who grow tobacco.

But it gets more personal than that.

I have a neighbor who runs a farm that adjoins mine at Elam, which is good tobacco country. This neighbor of mine doesn't smoke, for moral reasons, but he raises and sells several tons of tobacco per year.

I smoke, but I won't raise tobacco on my farm, for moral reasons.

So how come I'm the one that feels guilty?

November 19, 1979.
In the past, I think I have mentioned the congressional district work period in this space.

That is, for those of you unacquainted with the legislative process, a time when the Congress tears itself away from Washington and travels home to consult with the voters.

The House, for example, is taking this entire week as a district work period; never mind that some of us among the

41

citizenry will take a day off on Thanksgiving. Not those fellows, no sir, district work period all week.

I'd think they'd want to rest up a bit. After all they just had a district work day butted up against the Veterans' Day weekend, a week of district work period at Halloween.

And in about a month, another district work period around Christmas and New Year's staring them in the face.

I wonder if it isn't time we insist they stop being so hard on themselves.

December 6, 1979.

Washington, D.C., that wonderful city where logic is the rarest of diseases, has struck again.

Our nation's capital has passed a law, like most of the country has had for some time, permitting right turns on red lights.

However, there will not be much of a difference.

At least eighty percent of the intersections in Washington fall outside the federal guidelines where right turns on red are permitted.

These include intersections where there is significant potential for vehicular-pedestrian conflict; in English, that's a corner where there's lots of foot traffic, corners with poor visibility, and school zones.

No argument with that, you just put up signs permitting right turns on red at the twenty percent of intersections where such turns are advisable.

Don't you?

Certainly not.

You've already guessed the solution Washington came up with. You put "no right turn on red" signs at eighty percent of the street corners.

What's the difference?

A quarter of a million dollars or so; but the taxpayers will take care of that.

February 3, 1980.

Well, it seems the FBI may have caught several members of Congress with their morals down.

And, of course, a lot of people in high places are shocked, and surprised; they've said so.

Reminds me of the story my uncle used to tell about an English teacher whose husband caught her kissing another man.

"Woman, I'm surprised at you," he shouted.
"No," she replied, "you're shocked... I am the one who's surprised...."

February 5, 1980.
I was extremely interested yesterday in the story of Senator Larry Pressler. He's the Republican from South Dakota who had the opportunity to get in on some of the money in operation ABSCAM, but refused.

It's good to know Senator Pressler could not be bought.

It is, however, sad to note that the refusal of a United States Senator to take part in what he perceived to be an illegal operation is, in itself, a headline story.

There's nothing especially commendable about it.

That's the way senators and congressmen are *supposed* to act.

March 20, 1980.
Sometimes I feel guilty about the snide remarks I make from time to time about Congress.

Any fair observer should realize that these fellows, five hundred thirty-five if you count senators and congressmen together, have a very nearly impossible job.

Take this budget problem they're dealing with right now.

The President has given them the job of balancing the budget; and in order to do that they have to find over thirteen billion dollars that the federal government is now spending, that it doesn't need to spend.

About the only thing they know for sure right now is that the wasteful spending is taking place in somebody else's district.

March 25, 1980.
Senator William Proxmire's Golden Fleece Award has become an American institution.

Every so often he singles out a government project that spends the taxpayer's money and does something for the taxpayer that the taxpayer might be able to do without.

Like monkey research. A few years ago, Senator Proxmire landed on a Michigan professor for spending one half million dollars of our money finding out why monkeys grind their teeth.

Well, it seems the professor sued the senator, and won a ten-thousand-dollar settlement.

Senator Proxmire noted that he didn't do his research properly and announced that he would pay the ten thousand dollars out of his pocket. After all, it was his mistake.

What Senator Proxmire didn't mention was that the one hundred twenty-five thousand dollars in legal fees in the case came from the pockets of the good old American taxpayer.

It probably just slipped his mind.

March 26, 1980.

The Associated Press reported an interesting situation in Washington today.

It seems there's this union of government employees with about two thousand members and it's getting sick and tired of the way it's being treated by the federal agency its members work for.

It's working conditions mainly, says a union member, and the fact that the agency in question is exhibiting a complete disregard for the rights of its employees. Wages, of course, are set by Congress.

So the union will be picketing that agency in Washington and in thirty-three regional offices around the country.

The agency in question?

Would you believe, the National Labor Relations Board?

April 3, 1980.

It's possible that you have visited Washington, D.C. without having visited the National Visitors Center there.

The Visitors Center used to be a railroad station, but Congress spent twenty-one million of our tax dollars changing it into a visitors center which, for some reason, hardly anyone ever visits.

Anyway, last year as the Visitors Center was nearing completion, the House Public Works Committee decided to convert it back into a railroad station, and allowed as how it would take thirty-nine million of our dollars to do that.

That proposal died, so the Committee has renewed the proposal and lowered the price to thirty-six million.

So, for a total of fifty-seven million we get to take what was a railroad station and fashion it into a railroad station.

It makes another committee's funding of research into a

solar-heated doghouse look like a model of fiscal responsibility.

April 4, 1980.
A number of interesting notes on the wire today.
Government officials in Tucson, Arizona, solved a traffic problem.
This particular corner had generated a number of pedestrian accidents, such as one gentleman walking into a concrete pillar, another fellow running into a wall while skateboarding.
The problem wasn't on the sidewalk, it was inside the city library.
Specifically, the librarian, Kay Gregory.
More specifically, Kay Gregory's legs.
Legs which could be seen through the library window.
Legs that caused the following governmental memo to be written: Quote...Please cause the office furniture in the governmental reference library to be arranged in such a way as to minimize distractions to persons passing by the window ... Unquote.
That's what it said.
What it meant was, Kay Gregory's got a dynamite pair of legs.

April 21, 1980.
If the cost of vacations is getting you down, hang on for this one. The fifteen-cent stamp may soon be a thing of the past.
The Post Office folks say they need another five billion dollars a year to fight inflation, and they propose to get it by raising rates.
For you and me, the average letter writer, the stamp for a first class letter would go up a nickel, or about twenty-five percent, if my math is right.
For those wonderful folks who send us junk mail, advertisements for all sorts of things we probably don't need, and can't afford, the bill would go up two percent.
I'm sure that must be fair, or the postal service wouldn't have suggested it.

April 21, 1980.
On our earlier broadcast I noted the proposal by the postal service to increase the first class letter rate from fifteen

to twenty cents, and further noted that this constituted a twenty-five percent increase.

Of course five cents is twenty-five percent of twenty cents, but it's thirty-three and a third percent of fifteen cents. So a reasonable observer could claim that I made an error in calculation.

I've had several hours to ponder the situation and calls from a good many reasonable observers claiming I made an error in calculation.

So, I've decided to come clean.

My apparent error in math was merely an exercise in psychology. I wanted to see if you were paying attention.

And boy were you *ever* paying attention.

May 12, 1980.

I don't know if you've been keeping track or not, but I found out today that the Department of Health Education and Welfare which was recently denuded of its responsibility for education, is still using the old middle name.

I discovered that alarming fact in a story about consultants. Consultants, in the Washington sense, are people you hire to tell you how to go about keeping your job.

Anyway, in this story about consultants, HEW is still called Health-Education and Welfare.

Health-Education and Welfare, said the story, recently suspected that it had too many consultants on the payroll. So, to be sure, they hired a consultant to find out.

They estimate it'll take this consultant about forty thousand dollars to find out if there are too many other consultants.

In the meantime, I have a suggestion for how HEW can use the E for Education that no longer applies.

The word I had in mind was EXCESS.

May 19, 1980.

There's a deadline coming up according to the Internal Revenue Service.

It's June 1st.

Don't panic, there's not a new tax we hadn't heard about. June 1st is the deadline for us to file our comments with the IRS about tax forms, how we think they might be improved, made easier to understand and fill out.

But, our friendly IRS folks want us to understand that

they're only interested in our comments on the forms; on the tax, we should make those facts known to Congress.
Sorta takes the fun out, doesn't it?

June 2, 1980.
According to a little feature the Associated Press runs every day to keep us up to date, we've used up a hundred fifty-four days of 1980...leaving two hundred twelve in which to accomplish whatever we have plans to do with this particular year.

I would have figured that even Congress might be able to do something useful with two hundred twelve days; then I did some checking.

Those fellows on the Hill will take off:
nine days this month...
...eighteen days in July;
...twenty days in August;
...eight days in September.

And then it's time to adjourn and take to the campaign trail.

The way I figure it, Congress has—at a generous estimate—seventy-two days to deal with inflation, come up with an energy policy, address massive unemployment, tackle our Middle East and other foreign policies, and get re-elected.

That last item isn't a problem, though; that sort of work can even be done on one's day off.

June 5, 1980.
It's always nice to see Congress so sure of something.

The latest thing the Congress is sure of, by more than ten to one in the House, is that a ten cents tax on gasoline is no way to encourage Americans to conserve.

They've been equally sure that a rationing system isn't the way to do it either.

As a matter of fact, Congress has, over the months—no years—since most Americans realized we had an energy problem, come up with whole coveys of ways not to approach the problem.

We now have some pretty solid ideas from the Hill on how not to do it.

But I'm afraid the sixty-odd days those fellows plan to work for the balance of the year might not be enough to

explore the other side of the coin.
How to deal with energy.

June 9, 1980.

Mike Causey, who writes the Federal Diary column in the Washington *Post*, had an interesting revelation to make: The government is going to turn off the hot water in federal buildings.

Studies show that it will save ten thousand dollars a month for Uncle if some four hundred thousand federal workers wash their hands in cold water instead of hot.

Imagine that, ten thousand dollars a month.

Why, with money like that we can afford two or three more consultants to monitor paper clip flow at the Pentagon.

But that wasn't the real reason for the hot water cutoff. The real reason is to show those guys in the oil-producing nations that we're willing to sacrifice in order to convince them that we mean business.

They must be scared to death.

June 11, 1980.

Back in 1970 then postal employee William Hurst of Riverside, Missouri, wrote then President Richard Nixon an eight-page letter.

The letter was not complimentary, in fact it was littered with obscenities; and the post office reacted by firing Hurst.

Now, however, Hurst has successfully pressed his case in federal court, and has been awarded thirty-four thousand dollars in damages.

The federal judge pointed out that while Hurst was liberal with profanity in the letter to Nixon, that he did not threaten Nixon's life.

He might have added that the recipient of the letter was, as we later learned, not entirely unacquainted with the sort of language Hurst used. Of course, he lost his job too.

June 25, 1980.

I ran across some interesting figures today from a congressional hearing held yesterday.

The Department of Energy, which has twenty-one thousand employees, hires ten times that many people as outside contractors and consultants.

In another spot I learned that that same department has six people, that's six, not six hundred or six thousand, but six people assigned to handle hotlines and answer our questions on a number of energy-related subjects.

There's a hotline for questions about gasoline and heating oil.

One for information about alcohol fuels.

One to advise us, get this, on conservation.

Another for solar heating and cooling information.

And one to tell us how to go about car pooling.

Which, I suppose, is all very wonderful.

I could only wish, however, that they could add a seventh person, and a seventh hotline, to tell us what the devil we're paying two hundred twenty thousand nine hundred and ninety-three other people for.

September 10, 1980.

I have a feeling that the resistance to wider use of solar energy will diminish as the cost of other fuels goes up.

And, as we all know, the price of other fuels will go up.

Having seen a lot of different approaches to the use of solar energy, and most of them fairly simple, it's been a mystery to me why people aren't clamoring for it, demanding it, taking nothing less than the fullest advantage, especially in new construction.

A friend of mine says he knows why. Says it's too simple. People don't trust something that doesn't have some tubes, or transistors, or thermocouples.

But, just let the sun shine in and collect the heat, that's too simple.

Well sir, help is on the way.

Government and industry are working pell-mell to come up with ways to make the collection of solar energy complicated, and very expensive; and with any luck they'll figure out how to put a meter on it.

Why, in twenty years or so there may even be a solar cartel.

March 19, 1981.

Going through this year's federal budget isn't one of the most comforting things a taxpayer can do.

It tells, in mournful numbers, that everything costs more.

That isn't surprising, but the fact that bad news is expected doesn't make it any easier to take.

Well, I found a bright spot today—not much of a bright spot—but any port in a storm.

The House of Representatives this year will spend only about thirty-five and one-half million dollars on postage—about fifteen million dollars less than last year.

"Less," I said, "how can that be?"

Surely it has nothing to do with the fact that the members of the House don't stand for re-election this year ... Surely.

That's Thirteen News and a dash of cynicism.

July 8, 1981.

It's hard to believe that it was just a year ago today that the Republican Party was getting together on a platform for an upcoming election.

Somehow it seems that that campaign went on for years, and that it's been over for years. It just goes to show you how quickly things change.

Just a year ago, there was a question as to whether the Moral Majority would, or should, have an effect on the outcome of the election. Whether they did or not is a question that gets different answers, depending on *whom you ask.*

But it seems to me that in a democracy there's no question at all that people have a right to band together and involve themselves in politics to whatever extent they care to.

Where I part company with the Moral Majority is in the exercise of power without bothering to first get elected. Like, for instance, calling for President Reagan's new Supreme Court appointee to go before a Moral Majority panel, which would presumably determine her fitness to serve on the Court.

I believe the Constitution provides for the Senate to do that job; and, while they may not necessarily be right, they are elected, usually by a majority.

August 7, 1981.

I've been standing to one side in this air traffic controllers' issue, hoping that I might see a glimmer of hope that reason will prevail.

My problem is that I don't really agree with either side.

On the one hand, I don't believe one should strike if one has made a promise not to. On the other, if there's no other way of getting the government's attention, perhaps a strike was the practical if not completely legal thing to do.

So far, the whole mess has been handled badly. It sorta reminds me of the time in my youth when I drew a line in the dirt and dared Frankie Wells to step across.

When I drew the line I knew full well that Frankie would not step across that line. After all, I was a head taller than Frankie, and probably outweighed him.

Well, I don't exactly remember what caused me to draw that line in the first place, that is, what the original argument was about, but I do remember that Frankie stepped across the line and beat the tar out of me.

It has been my principle ever since then to negotiate, especially if I was not more sure of winning than I was the day Frankie beat me up.

In the controllers' matter, no matter who wins, there must have been a better way than drawing lines; now everybody's getting the same result—nowhere.

September 2, 1981.
There are some things about government and its many agencies, I suppose, that I will never understand.

Today I read in the Washington *Post* that the Food and Drug Administration is all upset about a product called "Indian Earth."

It was the first I'd heard about Indian Earth, but, as I understand it, it's sort of red dirt that is packaged in an earthenware pot and sold for twelve or fifteen dollars.

Also, as I understand it, women who can afford to pay twelve or fifteen dollars for this "Indian Earth" use it to color their faces.

If I'm not terribly mistaken, women have been using such substances for thousands of years. But now that it's being commercially marketed, the FDA wants it to stop. Not that it's dangerous, just that it hasn't been proved not to be dangerous.

On the other hand, we've been hearing a lot lately about counterfeit drugs deliberately made to look like illegal drugs that are being peddled to drug users.

There's good reason to believe that the counterfeits are

51

themselves dangerous, and especially so since they might cause a drug user to take an overdose of the real thing by accident.

But we're also told that the FDA, which can get excited about red dirt, can't get excited about dangerous drugs, if they're legal.

Like I said, there are some things I'll never understand.

CHAPTER 4

Sure enough...just as I predicted back in '79...the Democrats and Republicans fielded candidates in '80, and one of them got elected.
But it wasn't easy.
First, we all had to endure...

THE ENDLESS ELECTION YEAR

November 9, 1979.
During the last presidential election a friend of mine in Washington told me he could predict the outcome of the presidential election by counting bumper stickers.

His theory was that people who cover up the chrome on their cars are deeply committed.

Sure enough, some days before the election his bumper sticker poll showed that Jimmy Carter would win, and he did. So, I'm going to employ that theory this year, and let you know from time to time who's ahead.

Just now, after a preliminary poll at Military Circle it looks like a neck and neck race for second between Carter and Kennedy, with the Loch Ness Monster clearly in the lead.

January 4, 1980.
In the opinion of some of my colleagues, the President hurt himself badly tonight with the nation's farmers by imposing restrictions on grain sales to Russia.

I differ with them.

Farmers like to sell their product, true enough, but not to the benefit of our enemies.

In fact, back in the early seventies when grain sales to Russia were first in the works and being promoted by the Nixon Administration, it was farmers, not politicians, or newsmen, or the State Department, who suggested that this was a mistake.

I did a poll for ABC back then that comes ringing back to me now.

More than eighty percent of the farmers I interviewed expressed a single idea: If we help the Russians feed their people, they can turn their attention to armaments, and at the same time make their system appear to be more successful than it really is.

Jimmy Carter may lose the farm vote, but it won't be because he won't sell grain to the Russians.

January 8, 1980.

It's always been a source of wonder to me that anyone in his right mind would want to be president.

I spent a year as president of my high school latin club, and promptly, at the end of my first term, retired from elective politics forever.

But a great many apparently rational men and women do aspire to lead... and by some miracle, some of them wind up doing the job very well.

In the case of presidents, we're not terribly kind. We require them to make judgments, and take actions which, in the best of circumstances can be very difficult indeed. Then we hold them personally responsible for the aftereffects.

In the current situation, which is complicated and quite dangerous, that's probably not a fair requirement to put on another human being.

But it's part of the job description.

January 22, 1980.

The outcome in Iowa last night was interesting for a number of reasons.

It not only told us who the current front runners are but it also contained a political lesson for the politicians.

They were, if you remember, just about unanimous in the stated belief that the grain embargo against Russia was a political mistake.

They believed that Iowans, who depend very heavily on the farm economy, would resent the danger presented to their economy by the grain embargo.

They read, rightly, that the grain embargo would make things tough for the farmer, and for the many businesses and industries that depend on the farmer.

But they didn't listen closely enough.

The reading of the grain embargo by the people who stood to lose was that it would be difficult, not that it would be wrong.

March 11, 1980.
   Apathy is costly in more ways than one, but I suppose we are making some improvements in the democratic process.
   They used to tell the story down in Arkansas about two precinct workers who were out in a graveyard collecting names for an upcoming election.
   One fellow found a tombstone with a hyphenated name on it.
   Says to his co-worker, "Looky here, here's a fellow with two last names, reckon we can vote him twice?"
   "Nossir," says the other, "I ain't having nothing to do with a dishonest election."

March 11, 1980.
   The freedom we have in this country not to take part in the political process is one we seem to exercise all too often.
   That is, if we believe the figures.
   Try, for example, to find someone who did not vote in the last election.
   It's almost impossible.
   If you're talking to someone who doesn't like the way things are going, you'll find that he voted for the candidate or party that lost; and if he does like it, he voted for the winner.
   I suspected this to be the case some time ago, and took a poll.
   The results of the poll can now be made public.
   Henry Howell and Gerald Ford won in a landslide.

March 13, 1980
   President Carter's campaign organization is upset, we're told, because he wasn't invited to lead the St. Patrick's Day parade in Chicago, and Senator Kennedy was.
   Well, for one thing, the President hasn't been available for such events in recent days, so Mayor Byrne could be forgiven for thinking this would be no exception.
   But Mayor Byrne explains it this way....
   Senator Kennedy is Irish, and President Carter is English.
   Now it all makes sense.
   Of course, Chicago always has an Irishman at the head of the St. Patrick's Day parade. I checked. And prominent

55

figures in past St. Patrick's Day parades in Chicago have included such famous Irishmen as Franklin Roosevelt, Harry Truman, Adlai Stevenson, and Dan Ristenkowski.
Rules are rules.

March 18, 1980.
I was talking to a neighbor the other day about all these primary elections we have every election year, and how confusing it is.

This week we have one set of front runners, and next week another, with this week's leaders saying last week's results don't really mean anything anyway.

Anyway, my neighbor said he doesn't see why we don't just have one national primary to choose the nominees, and then a runoff if one's needed, and have done with it.

Says this would eliminate the confusion, the wheeling and dealing, much of the expense, and free the elected to work for the people, and the unelected from having to spend over a year wearing TV makeup.

I don't know if it's a solution or not, but it's a heck of a good description of the problem.

April 24, 1980.
I've been trying to remain very neutral on the question of the presidential candidates.

For one thing, it's none of my business how anyone else votes, nor is it my place to try to influence anyone to vote one way or the other.

But I also don't want to appear unconcerned about the leadership of my country and yours.

So, I'd like to declare myself once and for all, and get it over with.

I stand firmly with the man who believes America should reassert its leadership in the world, for the man whose economic policies have proved successful, for the man with a proven record of success in the face of uncertain conditions, for the man whose understanding of the difficulties in the Middle East, and ability to manage them, is unfailingly right, and has provided his constituents with prosperity.

Only trouble is, I don't think we can hire him away from Exxon.

May 30, 1980.
Back during the 1972 presidential campaign I was assigned by ABC to cover the election from Columbus, Ohio.

With just the right mixture of dependence on agriculture, business, and industry, Columbus seemed, to us, sort of a small model of the American people as a whole; and indeed, it turned out that way. The final vote count in Columbus was just a couple of percentage points away from the national result.

So, I was interested in the popular response in Columbus yesterday when President Carter and Governor Reagan held rallies there.

Between the two of them they drew less than thirteen thousand people.

David Broder of the Washington *Post* put that into perspective.

Says Broder, these two mighty machines turned out about one sixth the number that Ohio State's football team draws for a non-conference game on a rainy Saturday afternoon at the beginning of hunting season.

June 13, 1980.
This being the last day of school for many youngsters in this area, it would be hard to convince them that there's anything unlucky about Friday the 13th.

As for me, I'm not superstitious.

It doesn't bother me to spill salt, or break a mirror; I've been known to walk under ladders, and get away with it.

I've gone through a pretty lucky lifetime without ever owning a rabbit's foot or a four-leaf clover.

So, I'm certainly not going to get upset about a mere day like Friday the 13th.

I just can't be convinced that there's anything unlucky about any particular day.

With the possible exception of November 4th.

June 25, 1980.
You've probably heard by now that there's a new dictionary out that makes the November election in this country unnecessary.

Webster's Encyclopedic Dictionary, with fifty thousand copies already in print lists the fortieth president of the

57

United States as Ronald Reagan.

Ronald Wilson Reagan, to be specific.

The folks at Webster's say they're embarrassed, but not embarrassed enough to take the loss on fifty thousand dictionaries and withdraw them from the market.

So now, we not only know who the fortieth president will be, but also that he has a middle name—and that his last name is pronounced Regan, or is it Reegan?

It could be the biggest thing since the election of Thomas Dewey.

July 10, 1980.

In one of his books, *I Love You I Hate You,* Guy Friddell advances the theory that politicians are people just like the rest of us.

Well, I don't completely agree, but I must admit that the Republican Platform Committee has indicated some substance in Friddell's theory.

Taking a firm stand, sort of, on both sides of the Equal Rights Amendment fight, those Republicans reminded me a little of my big brother Bill. He's a judge now, and he was a judge when I was eight, and he was fourteen.

Considering his age to be reason for authority, I once took a dispute to him, a dispute I was having with a neighbor boy. He listened carefully to both cases, then rendered his decision with Solomon like wisdom.

"Go outside and fight it out...."

I didn't discover until yesterday that he was probably destined to become a Republican.

July 14, 1980.

According to an article in *People* magazine, the upcoming presidential campaign may get pretty dirty.

The person quoted in the article says the Republicans are not all that high-minded and will be able to sling mud, to trip, and scratch, even—heaven forfend—hit below the belt.

That opinion was not rendered by a Democrat, or even an Independent.

That opinion was rendered by Maureen Reagan, the thirty-nine-year-old daughter of a prominent Republican named Ronald Reagan.

It could be that she's running for the Billy Carter Diplomacy Award.

July 15, 1980.
It's been suggested that the Republican Convention, now in progress, and the upcoming Democratic Convention next month, constitute an enormous waste of time.

After all, the detractors say, we know who the nominees will be, we know essentially that each party will promise to cure the country's ills in a fashion far more reasonable and true to the American way of life than the other party.

But there is a purpose to be served.

These conventions provide a perfect excuse for the nation's legislature to spend most of July and August somewhere other than Washington.

If you've ever spent a day on Capitol Hill in July or August when the legislature is in session, you know that holding political conventions as an excuse to recess can only be regarded as a humanitarian act.

July 16, 1980.
Most of the talk around the convention in Detroit today is whether former President Ford will be Ronald Reagan's running mate.

And naturally, the journalism fraternity is trying to sort out the rumors and get down to the facts.

Here's what we know so far.

The Reagan camp says it has not offered Ford the vice-presidential spot.

The Ford camp said the Reagan camp did offer the job, but Ford turned it down, said to get Bush instead.

Betty Ford said she wouldn't put any odds on it either way, but wouldn't rule it out.

Reagan himself says he hasn't decided yet.

Ford himself says he's not seeking the nomination.

As you can see, there's a lot of news there but no information, and I'm told that there are almost as many newspersons in Detroit this week as there are Republicans.

July 18, 1980.
It warmed my heart to be able to not go to the Republican Convention this year.

I plan to enjoy the Democratic Convention equally as much, since I don't have to go to that one either.

About the only thing I don't like about John Anderson is the fact that the Independents are not having a convention for me not to have to go to.

The trouble with conventions is that they're always held at the hottest time of the year, and so is most of the campaign that follows; and the honor of being one of the reporters following the action can be a dubious one when you're soaked with sweat one minute, and freezing to death in an air-conditioned room the next.

It plays hob with your objectivity.

I believe in the system, but I must admit that a time or two in 1976 I was sorry we'd done away with a hereditary monarchy.

August 1, 1980.

A viewer called the other day to complain. And the point he made was certainly valid.

This person contended that the use of the word—and I'll admit up front that it's a silly word—that the use of the word "Billygate" is unfair.

For one thing, the gate syllable makes it seem that this scandal is as serious as Watergate was, which it probably isn't.

Well, I won't argue with that, but I know how the Washington press corps thinks. I used to be a member of it.

The reason for the almost immediate coining of the word Billygate is as follows: It's one word. It takes up just a tiny amount of newspaper space, and takes about a quarter to a third of a second to say aloud on a television report.

On the other hand, "A scandal involving Billy Carter's connections with the Libyan government and the possible effect this might have on the conduct of American foreign policy . . ." takes five lines of copy. Or about seven seconds that could be used for juicy detail.

That's the reason.

Not a very good one I guess.

But it is the reason.

August 5, 1980.

Fair's fair. So the next time a Republican says to you that the Democrats are taxing us to death, just snap right back that it was the Republicans who started the income tax anyway.

A hundred and nineteen years ago today, Abraham Lincoln signed a measure into law that taxed American

incomes over eight hundred dollars at the rate of three percent.
The Union needed the money to raise an army to handle the Great Unpleasantness with the Confederacy.
That income tax was rescinded ten years later of course, and it was some time before the Sixteenth Amendment came along to enrich our lives.
So, like I said, it's only fair to blame the Republicans for the whole idea of an income tax.
It took the Democrats, of course, to turn it into an American art form.

August 8, 1980
One of my chief regrets at the coming of the Democratic Convention next Monday is that Finley Peter Dunne is not around to cover it.
Dunne, of course, went to his reward in 1936 and took his creation, Mister Dooley, with him. Mister Dooley was the political observer who first remarked, in an Irish brogue, that "The Demmycratic Party ain't on speakin' terms with itself."
How timeless that statement turns out to be.
With the choices we have this year, another of Mister Dooley's observations seems to apply.
He said, the man that would expect to train a lobster to fly is called a lunatic, but a man that thinks men can be turned into angels by an election is called a reformer—and remains at large.

August 11, 1980.
Well, it's under way, and the fighting should start in earnest in a couple of hours or so.
After the drama at the Republican Convention over whether former President Ford would be on the ticket, some folks thought the Democratic Convention would be a dull affair.
After all, President Carter has the nomination locked up. Just about everybody but Ted Kennedy believes that, and we already know who his running mate will be.
Fritz Mondale, of course, unless lightning strikes and the delegates actually do vote to open the convention, in which case we could really have a show this week.
Actually, it was H. L. Mencken who noted the major

difference between Republicans and Democrats—and we should see it demonstrated four nights running.

Democrats, said Mencken, are louder and they sweat more.

August 12, 1980.

In my youth down in Arkansas everyone who belonged to a political party was a Democrat.

Oh, I suppose there were some Republicans, but they kept quiet about it.

So, with all that Democratic tradition behind me I think I have a right to say that I'm disappointed in the Democrats something fierce.

Here they had all the makings of a good fight, a real donnybrook, and they blew it in less than two hours.

Now, with the presidential and vice presidential nominations all set, the only mystery is whether Senator Kennedy will show up Thursday night to stand side by side with President Carter in his moment of glory.

As mysteries go it's a little boring.

No, I take that back, it's a lot boring.

It's like watching a horse race between Genuine Risk and a couple of draft horses.

August 13, 1980.

Ted Kennedy made a great speech last night. He made some telling points, and as usual, with eloquence. He's a marvelous speaker.

So, I'll give him an A for oratory.

On another matter, freedom of speech, give Teddy an F. He said Ronald Reagan had no right to quote Franklin Roosevelt.

Well, it was probably a poor choice of words.

He must have meant that Reagan shouldn't quote Roosevelt, or that it was hypocritical for Reagan to quote Roosevelt, or that it was impolite for Reagan to quote Roosevelt.

But, after all, Ronald Reagan has the right to quote anybody he jolly well pleases to quote.

The First Amendment guarantees that.

Even a politician should know that.

August 14, 1980.
   Well, the convention ends tonight, President Carter will accept the nomination we've all known he'd get since June 3rd, the day the primary system sent him over the top.
   But we have learned some things.
   We've learned that the terms acclamation and unanimous are far different in meaning.
   We've learned that normally sane people will wear just about anything on their heads to advertise their loyalty to a political candidate.
   We've learned that the "Star Spangled Banner" is not one of Willie Nelson's better songs.
   We've learned that zealous reporters can search for hours and days for answers to questions we probably would never have asked in the first place.
   And we've learned, or should have, that this one and the Republican Convention could have probably accomplished the actual work of their four-day extravaganzas by mail.

September 22, 1980.
   Now that the first debate is history, the debate will begin over whether this candidate or that one won, what effect it will have on the President's candidacy that he didn't show up? Whether Reagan's conservatism or Anderson's liberalism will carry the day? All sorts of questions.
   We'll get the answers in a few days, of course.
   Carter's polls will tell us that the American people agree with his decision not to participate in a debate with a third party candidate who can't win anyway.
   Anderson's polls will tell us that if all the people who won't vote for Anderson because he can't win would vote for Anderson, that he could win.
   And Reagan's polls will tell us that we should pay no attention to the things the Carter and Anderson polls tell us.
   And then there will be all the independent polls that will tell us, "See there...We told you so...."
   What we really need is fewer polls telling us what we think, or worse, what to think, but more thinking and more participation in the poll that counts, November 4th.

September 30, 1980.
   This is a sort of off time of the year—there's not a really big general holiday to celebrate till Halloween, and that's a month away.

So, to fill in the time, I'd like to remind you of some smaller, more specialized celebrations available between now and then—enough, perhaps, to hold us till Columbus Day anyway.

This is National Chimney Sweep Week, tomorrow is Botswana Day and the beginning of National Needlework Week, Chow Mein Month, Gourmet Adventure Month, National Apple Jack Month, Pizza Month, and World Vegetarian Day.

It's also President Carter's birthday.

And that reminds us that there are only thirty-five more shopping days until November 4th.

October 1, 1980.

It's a curious thing that happens to people in positions of great influence.

Our Congress, for example, is having such a hard time getting along with itself that it was unable, over the course of the last fiscal year, to come up with a funding bill for this fiscal year.

It seems that such an important bill is often used to ride some other legislation through that otherwise wouldn't pass.

Then there are the debates.

Carter won't attend a debate that includes Anderson, Reagan won't go to one that doesn't include Anderson.

Did it ever occur to you that if our kids acted like our national leaders, we'd probably be tempted to spank them and send them to bed without their supper.

October 14, 1980.

The polls keep coming out, faster in fact than we can keep up with them.

They say Carter's winning here, Reagan there; Anderson has no chance but could be a spoiler.

Well, I've decided to ignore the polls from now on. Even the speeches and the claims made by the supporters. I've decided to turn to more scientific methods of predicting the presidential winner.

And today, based on careful research into the results of the last nineteen presidential contests, I can confidently predict that Ronald Reagan will be elected.

He's four inches taller than Jimmy Carter.

In eighteen of the past nineteen elections the taller candidate won.

The single exception was last time, when Jimmy Carter beat Gerald Ford in spite of a three-inch height advantage on Ford's part.

Maybe he can do it again, but I just can't resist eighteen to one odds and a height spread of four inches.

October 22, 1980.

Decision time draws ever nearer, and many of us are still on the fence.

I spoke to a lady on the phone today who said she's finally made up her mind.

She's voting for the man, she said, who promises a tax cut, to keep us out of war, but strong among nations; to solve the economic problems of inflation, recession, and high unemployment; to take the high road in dealing with political opponents; to deal effectively with the Soviet Union; to expand trade with China; to keep the peace in the Middle East; and just generally fulfill the American Dream.

She never did say whom she had in mind.

October 24, 1980.

Well, sir we've got just a matter of days to make up our minds.

Nobody ever said it would be easy.

But, I kept my eye on the television tonight and finally came to a decision.

Admittedly, I was already inclined in certain directions, but tried to keep an open mind about things until the very last to weigh all the factors in the equation, to balance all the pros and cons, to make a decision based more on facts than on mere emotion or gut reaction.

But, for better or worse, the die is cast, I have decided.

And I think I'll reveal my decision for all to hear and evaluate.

Mind you, I don't want to influence anyone else's decision, but this year I'm going trick or treating as the Frankenstein monster.

October 28, 1980.

Some of the preliminary ballyhoo around tonight's debate makes it sound more like a championship prize fight than a serious forum.

In this corner, jolting Jimmy Carter, putting his title on the line against rough Ronnie Reagan.

Carter clearly has his opponent shaded in terms of age—he has less of it—and experience, he has more of it. But, rightly or wrongly, he's picked up the reputation for being willing to fight dirty when he's in trouble.

Reagan, on the other hand, has possibly the better ring moves because of his movie experience, a factor that may work for, or against him, depending on the underdog factor.

Ninety minutes of verbal sparring, ladies and gentlemen, when the main event begins.

It's almost sure to go the distance, neither of these guys has a knockout issue.

And the judges' decision will be final—one week from today.

October 29, 1980.

If you watched the Big Debate on ABC last night, you know that for fifty cents a call viewers were invited to phone in their opinion on whether President Carter or Ronald Reagan got the best of the exchange.

If you acted on the offer, you may possibly have learned that it was not without its faults.

Some folks dialed Carter and got Reagan, some the other way around, though the telephone folks say the votes were cast correctly.

Some folks wound up talking to a pizza carryout in New Jersey.

A California police department got some of the calls.

But nearly seven hundred thousand calls did get through and were duly counted, and expressed a collective opinion that Reagan won—the breakdown was about two to one.

My own feeling was that they evaded the questions equally well.

And, at fifty cents a head, the phone company didn't do too badly either.

November 3, 1980.

Well, we have just a matter of hours left to make, change, or rethink our decisions on who shall lead the nation for the next four years.

Depending on whom you talk to, this has been the most

crucial, or the most unimportant election in years, the liveliest, or the most boring.

One thing we can all probably agree on, it's been the longest.

It seems like forever and then some.

And with a certain weariness of politics, I'd like to make you just one more election year promise.

If Jimmy Carter wins, I promise not to speculate on whether he'll be succeeded by Ted Kennedy or Fritz Mondale for at least a year.

If, on the other hand, Ronald Reagan wins—I will avoid discussing the possibility of a second term for that same year.

I know it's not much of a promise, but it may be the only one you'll get that will be kept.

November 7, 1980.

Just a few post election notes that you might have missed.

Harold Stassen, who's been running for President and losing since 1948, says this was his last campaign.

In the network race, CBS won with the most viewers, ABC won with the largest increase in viewers, and NBC predicted the outcome earliest.

A little something for everybody.

In the House, Senate, and Governor's races around the country you might be interested in the fact that Pickle and Pepper won, but Bacon, Rice, and Turnipseed lost; Lee won, but Grant lost; Chappel won, Church lost; Gray, White, and Brown won; but Black and Green lost; Kindness was a winner, but Hope lost; Crane and Fish were winners; but Canary, Fox, Wolf, and Beaver lost.

And Icenhouer was a winner and Dixon lost.

And finally, the town of Reagan, Indiana, voted solidly for Carter.

November 12, 1980.

Having lived for a number of years in Washington, I have a habit of reading the Washington *Post* every day.

For one thing, it makes me glad I don't have to live in Washington any more.

For another, I get to find out what a good many of my friends and colleagues are worrying about.

They're always worried, mind you, it's just that their

worries change like fashions.

Sometimes I wonder if the very act of political worrying isn't more a matter of what it's fashionable to worry about, than what it's logical to worry about.

Just now it's fashionable to worry about what will happen when President-elect Reagan puts his administration to work.

All the liberals are worried that it will be a too conservative administration, all the conservatives are worried that it will be too liberal.

And the radicals are already wearing "Impeach Reagan" T-shirts.

November 17 1980.
I think we've got a little case of poetic justice going here.

As you know, on election day, the folks out West knew who had won the presidency long before the polls were closed in their states—a fact that greatly upset some people running for office.

It was believed that the early knowledge of the inevitable outcome simply destroyed the will to vote in the western time zones. The networks, of course, pooh-poohed the idea, said the American voter is more sophisticated than that.

Well now, in a few days, when CBS finally gets around to airing the episode of Dallas in which the world learns who shot J. R.—that episode will air here in the East several hours before it airs in the western states.

Now CBS executives are afraid their ratings will suffer, that the word on who shot J. R. will get out, and Westerners will lose interest and watch something else.

I've been around the world three times, and I believe, that's the saddest story I've ever heard.

November 21, 1980.
It's all the rage in the nation's capital—a new book—just in time for Christmas.

It's a dry book, according to some who have read it; but the publisher says it sold over seventeen hundred copies the very first day on the market; and it's back-ordered, by the hundreds, at six dollars a copy.

The author, not the former mistress of a congressman, not a former White House aide now willing to tell all, not an undercover agent.

No sir, this one-hundred-sixty-one-page book that has Washington agog was written by none other than the House Committee on Post Office and Civil Service.

It's a list of jobs President-elect Reagan may fill, thousands of them.

Republicans call it the Plum Book.

Democrats say it isn't nearly as good as the one that came out four years ago.

CHAPTER 5

In the course of several years in the Army, and too many years chasing stories, and some traveling just for fun, I've logged forty-three countries into my experience, and I'm glad I went.

The best of them came close to measuring up to my standards, and the worst of them proved to me how valuable those standards are to me.

If someone were to accuse me of being a chauvinist, I'd just have to plead guilty.

There are places on this earth, I'm told, where the imperfections and contradictions that mark our American society are not allowed to exist. Like freedom, they have been legislated and regulated away, and their constitutions declare as much. Visiting, yes....

BUT I WOULDN'T WANT TO LIVE THERE

November 2, 1979.

I gained some moral assistance from an unusual quarter today.

Pearl Bailey....

It works this way. My wife grew up in that part of Luxembourg that identifies with France.

Therefore she cooks in the French fashion, which is good. But she also describes the dishes in French, which is bad.

I never know what's for dinner until I get there. I always enjoy it but I can't pronounce it. Until recently I thought "coq-au-vin" was some sort of chocolate dish. Imagine my surprise when it turned out to be chicken.

So, how does Pearl Bailey figure in all this?

Well, Pearl recently signed up for some courses at Georgetown University. Originally, she took French, but dropped that course and took theology instead.

Says God is easier to understand than French.

I couldn't have said it better myself.

January 9, 1980.

The Soviet Union is currently rounding up the dissatisfied residents of Moscow and moving them to areas of the country where western Olympic tourists will not go.

The Soviet Union has raised the prices on tourism, in advance of the Games, and arranged the rules in such a way that it will be very hard for any tourist to get there, or leave, without contributing a young fortune to the socialist paradise.

The Soviet Union has always violated the rules against professionalism in sports; it's simple, you go ahead and do it and call it something else. The same rule applies when you invade other countries.

It would be nice if the world of sport could be separate from politics. But it isn't, and certainly not under the Soviet system. It's sport for us, it's a propaganda show for them; and we pay the bill for both.

I don't like the idea of withdrawing from the Olympics.

But I like even less the fact that participating puts a certain stamp of respectability on a state that has proved it doesn't deserve it.

January 17, 1980.

Today, as you may recall, is Benjamin Franklin's birthday; and when such a figure's birthday comes along, I often indulge in a common exercise—that of wondering what he might have to say about the current state of affairs.

I ran across a quote immediately that seemed to be perfectly tailored to the news, that our ally Japan, which owes much of its success as an economic power to us, finds it cannot go along with sanctions against Iran or economic pressure on the Soviet Union.

Franklin's words: those who would give up a little liberty, for safety, deserve neither liberty nor safety.

January 23, 1980.

There was an interesting story in the business section of the Washington *Post* today.

It said the Commerce Department is currently considering some exceptions to the President's ban on selling high technology items to the Soviet Union.

It said some business people have been told they can do business as usual in about a month.

The Commerce Department explains this in a curious way.

The official statement says, and I quote, "It can reasonably be concluded that a policy of granting exceptions falling into a few hardship categories would not contravene the

President's wishes...."
In other words, it's okay to ask sacrifices of farmers and athletes, but business is business.

January 24, 1980.
I read a lengthy article today about the years of training and self-denial that it takes to become an Olympic athlete.

It went on about the deep worry of many of our American athletes that their chance to compete in Moscow may be taken away, and I sympathized with the young people involved.

I sympathized up to the point that a gymnastics coach was quoted, saying that those of us outside the athletic world can't realize just what it means to see your nation's flag raised in triumph.

Perhaps not, but I know where we can get the information.

In the wards of any veterans' hospital, for a start, or on a stroll through a military cemetery.

Such an exercise might also remind the interested visitor of what sort of self-denial it took to make the flag a triumphant symbol in the first place.

January 31, 1980.
The Washington *Post* carried a lengthy article today about some of the finer restaurants in the nation's capital, and how their owners are wrestling with a very heavy question: Whether to boycott caviar.

Most caviar, as you know, comes from Russia, or Iran.

Actually, it comes from the sturgeon, which swims in the Caspian Sea, which is robbed of its eggs by Russians and Iranians, who, not satisfied with one act of robbery, sell it to folks who believe there is something so special about it that it's worth thirty-five dollars an ounce.

The headwaiter at the Sans Souci said caviar should not be confused with politics.

Maybe so, but they do smell somewhat the same.

February 5, 1980.
It isn't Muhammad Ali's fault that he isn't a diplomat. In his chosen career, one in which he performed with great skill for great profit, diplomacy played hardly any part at all.

But the performance in Africa is disappointing.

Ali is no stranger to political dissent. He suffered because of his views, but only temporarily. He was, in the end, allowed to recover, and pile one success on top of another to a degree that few people enjoy in any society.

But the bulk of Ali's training and skill lies in fighting hard, but clean. Apparently, nobody told him those rules don't apply in international politics.

That was unfair—to Ali, and to the rest of us.

February 25, 1980.

There have been several stories in the news lately about this firm and that in the business of making sports equipment or clothes, that stands to lose a bundle because of the boycott of the summer Olympics in Moscow.

But, if you are feeling sorry for the Gym-Kyn firm in Reading, Pennsylvania, forget it.

Good old American ingenuity has saved the day.

The Gym-Kyn folks had made up a half million dollars worth of leotards and skating outfits with the Moscow Olympics logo on the front. Orders were cancelled by the thousands, of course.

So, they just printed the word "boycott" across that logo; and guess what: orders are coming in by the thousands.

March 27, 1980.

The Soviet Union is really miffed because we are using the Olympic Games as a political weapon. That's unheard of. One doesn't mix sport and politics, and besides, Afghanistan is none of our business.

But let's look at the record.

For thirty-four years the Russians stayed away from the Olympic Games because they were bourgeois.

They've boycotted dozens of international sports events because they were to be held in Chile, Spain, South Africa, and other countries, or stayed away because they didn't like the name some countries played under, or the politics of the participants.

But that's different, they'll explain.

You see, tovarisch, that was before the Olympic Games were scheduled to be played in Moscow.

March 27, 1980.

Up until today my personal sports heroes were few. In

fact, Mookie Wilson was about the entire list. But today I added a name, and for a good reason.

Nancy Lieberman, who's won enough honors not to need any from me, gets my vote as the sportsperson of the year.

Not only does Nancy state that she will support her country's policy on a boycott of the Olympics, she also points out why many other athletes don't.

It is a heavy sacrifice, the abandonment of a chance to be a national hero, perhaps... perhaps the chance to turn that fame into a lucrative professional career.

Nancy Lieberman wants to go to the Olympics; but, if it comes to that she says, and I quote, "I have to put my country before my individual interest."

And that's about as good a definition of patriotism as we're likely to hear in the age of me-ism.

April 8, 1980.

I see where the official Soviet news agency has accused the United States of playing politics with sport in calling for a boycott of the Moscow Olympics.

Well, I'd like to read you something: Quote... The view popular in the West that sport is outside politics finds no support in this country. Whenever someone says that sport lies outside the framework of political relations, we feel the remark is not a serious one... Unquote.

That is a paragraph from *Soviet Sport,* the official handbook for Soviet athletes.

A number of American athletes have complained that President Carter is using them as pawns.

I disagree, but even if it's so, I wonder if there's greater honor to be won by being used as pawns by the Soviet Union.

April 14, 1980.

Some energy-saving ideas came in from abroad today.

In England, a discovery by some school children that one may save energy by taking six minutes to make three-minute eggs.

It's this way, you just bring the water to a boil, then turn off the burner, drop in the egg, and wait six minutes.

Authorities say it could save Britain over six million dollars a year in energy costs.

In Thailand, the energy department says the elimination of television broadcasting in the evening will save Thailand

enormous amounts of money.
Thailand's director of family planning says it won't.

May 5, 1980.
The Cuban exodus continues and the reactions in this country vary.
Some folks believe Castro is probably using the flood of refugees to smuggle secret agents into the United States. Others figure he's emptying the jails, and just sending us the bottom rung of Cuban society. Still others say we're overpopulated already and simply don't have room for these new thousands.
And all these are good arguments, substantial arguments.
Accepting the thousands from other shores who continually come to us, looking for something they can't find at home, something so precious they seem willing to take any chance, make any sacrifice.
It's bad business all right and we probably ought to put a stop to it.
Now then, who wants to be the first to rewrite the rules?

May 13, 1980.
The French, you might have heard, have decided that the Russian invasion of Afghanistan is not reason enough to go along with a boycott of the Moscow Olympics.
But, if France is willing to play games with the Russians, Ed Allen is not.
Ed Allen is the head man at New Kent County's Annual International Bluegrass and Frog Hopping Hoedown.
It's sort of a counter event that happens the same weekend the frog jumping contest takes place in Calaveras County, California.
That's this weekend, and New Kent County expects to welcome competing frogs from England, Germany, France, Canada, Sweden, and most of the States.
Russian frogs, however, need not apply.

July 14, 1980.
I was set upon today by a Francophile to note that today was, after all, Bastille Day, a day as full of meaning for the French patriot as the Fourth of July is for us.
This particular person also knows that I am always miffed at the French about something—most lately the fact

that they're going to the Olympic Games.

But the French are, after all, a people of great courage and tenacity; their dedication to liberty and equality is as fierce as our own.

And I must admit also that part of my objection to the French probably stems from the fact that they have a perfectly beautiful language that I cannot learn, no matter how hard I try.

So, in fairness, and in honor of Bastille Day, I will say something positive about the French.

Here goes....

They showed remarkably good taste in selecting the colors for their flag.

There....

CHAPTER 6

Remember how angry we all were when a mob took our diplomats hostage in Iran?

At first we believed it was just a mob, and that Iran's new government was cautious, or cowardly, or just ineffective.

Then, when the truth dawned, that a mad mullah had corrupted Islamic morality to justify this crime, our national blood pressure went off the scale.

For four hundred and forty-four terrible days we were....

ALL HELD HOSTAGE

November 13, 1979.

Indignation at the Iranian taking of hostages continues to grow in this country; longshoremen won't service Iranian ships, airport workers won't work on Iranian airplanes, and American students are getting back into the business of conducting demonstrations.

But support for the release of hostages came from a decidedly unexpected quarter today.

There's a sign outside the Mustang Ranch in Reno, Nevada, today saying that that establishment will accept no more Iranian customers.

The Mustang Ranch employs about fifty practitioners of what is generally regarded as the world's oldest profession.

November 14, 1979.

The government of Iran decided today to withdraw the money it keeps in American banks.

The government of the United States shortly thereafter froze the assets of the Iranian government.

Guess what the official Iranian government response is to that act?

They say it's illegal.

Mind you, a government that is currently holding the lives of more than fifty human beings hostage, dares to call the holding of money illegal.

It took me, incredibly, back to my school days in Arkansas when I got a failing grade on an English composition.

The teacher explained it this way: Young man, he said,

before you use a word you owe it to your reader and to yourself to determine beforehand just what that word means.

November 14, 1980.
　I read with interest today an article describing a study of the personality of the Ayatollah Khomeini.
　The study notes that he was not open to the idea of bargaining, that he sees things in terms of what he personally determines is the will of God, and there's no room in that equation for any argument whatever.
　It was a scholarly study, I'm sure; but I came away from the article feeling that I had seen a description of such a person more plainly drawn...and I had.
　Finley Peter Dunn's character Mister Dooley said it....
　He said, a fanatic is a person who does what he thinks God would do if God had all the facts of the matter.

November 21, 1979.
　As the situation grows more serious, it's to be expected that our anger and frustration will grow as well.
　But a conversation I had today with an Iranian convinced me that some of our anger might well be just what the Ayatollah had in mind.
　Suppose our system allowed for hasty action and we simply rounded up Iranians wholesale, as some have suggested, and sent them home.
　It would have given the mob currently in control of Iran access to many of its enemies and to thousands who have seen our system in action, who might well compare it to a system which has one freedom, that being the freedom to agree with the head man.
　Luckily, our clumsy old democracy moves slowly and deliberately when it comes to applying justice, and with luck, we won't turn our backs on those who need and deserve our protection.
　So, doesn't it behoove us to be careful and direct our anger only at those who earn it?
　And shouldn't we be duly thankful that ours is the country and system people usually choose when they need something to escape to?
　We must be doing something right.

December 4, 1979.
   I suppose Jefferson might be upset with a lot of what he'd find today; but then he might be pleased too, to find that most of his theories on democracy, and tyranny have held up very well indeed.
   This week, in what passed for an expression of the will of the Iranian people, they placed their fate in the hands of one man.
   The Ayatollah Khomeini has proved himself to be a liar over and over again, he has abandoned all civilized principle; and we must assume, the people of Iran will now hear what he wants them to hear, and nothing else.
   Jefferson described the fate of such a society in a letter to a friend....
   He said, if a nation expects to be ignorant and free, in a state of civilization, it expects what never was—and never will be.

December 5, 1979.
   The question has been raised in recent days whether we should give either temporary, or permanent, asylum to a man such as the Shah of Iran.
   And the fact that the question has been raised has been enormously helpful...to those Iranians who are holding Americans hostage and to the leaders of that unhappy nation who scream for justice while engaging in the commission of a crime.
   Frankly, I have not seen hard evidence that the Shah was the tyrant the Ayatollah says he was.
   I suspect he might have been.
   But I do know about the Ayatollah, the drumhead trials, summary executions, and now the taking of hostages in defiance of international law, custom, and common human decency.
   Personally, I have little use for evidence from such a source, on the Shah, or any other subject.
   It's especially distressing to learn that a presidential candidate in this country has given Iran's new tyrant the impression that we may be prepared to accept his unacceptable point of view.

December 12, 1979.
  High school rallies....
  Christmas cards by the thousands....
  It's all happening here, and all over the country, as Americans express their feeling for fifty-two fellow Americans they don't even know by name.
  Word came today that the mail to the hostages, numbering in the hundreds of thousands of pieces, is now beginning to put a strain on the Iranian postal system.
  It must seem somewhat strange to the Iranians that so many can be so concerned about so few.
  But it could be the same effect that occurred in my family and, I suspect, in yours when we were young.
  I have a big brother named Bill. Sometimes, Bill thumped me pretty good. But if a neighbor kid tried to thump me, he had to reckon with Bill.

December 13, 1979.
  The Ayatollah Khomeini, I understand, is giving the United States credit for a demonstration today.
  It seems about a half million people marched in the streets of Tabriz, Iran, in opposition to Khomeini's so-called Islamic Constitution.
  But, he has remained strangely quiet about a demonstration for which our country is responsible.
  American postal authorities noted that mail addressed to the American hostages is increasing by the day.
  No less than forty thousand pieces went through JFK Airport in New York yesterday, and that nearly doubled to more than seventy thousand today.
  The address is simple: The Hostages, American Embassy, Teheran, Iran.
  Thirty-one cents gets a half-ounce letter or card there by air mail; and the post office says it's being forgiving if the postage is a little short.
  They may not be delivered, but somebody's going to have to deal with them.

December 14, 1979.
  There was a new broadside from Iran today, from what passes for a government, suggesting a new set of solutions for the impasse in Teheran.
  First, we must find the Shah guilty of crimes, then try him for those crimes, and gather his fortune and send it back to Iran.

But there was another message from Iran as well, to the United Nations, demanding that that body do something about American anger in this country, and what the message calls the harassment of Iranians here.

Well, as far as I know, except for less than a half dozen cases where violence was involved, no mass arrests have taken place.

But I'm having a hard time summoning up sympathy for those guests in our country who seem to demand the hospitality of a civilized country on the one hand, and condone publicly actions by their own government, if you can call a mob a government, which are clearly unacceptable in any civilized society.

It would behoove us to be good hosts, as we have been....

It would behoove our guests to behave themselves accordingly or go home to their own country, and their own century.

December 18, 1979.

Today, Americans observed Unity Day; some flew flags, some rang bells, wrote little encouraging notes in Christmas cards to the hostages, some prayed, some cursed Khomeini and all he stands for.

I suppose we were unified, today, but it wasn't anything we had to be goaded into.

We've been sharing an ever-growing sense of indignation and frustration for forty-five days now, most of us.

Certainly, our holidays are not as happy as they might be, and most of us think a lot about how terrible it is for the hostages themselves, and their families.

And...there's very little comfort to be found for the situation, unless maybe it's a rediscovery of something the rest of the world has known for a long time, whether they like it or not.

Our system isn't perfect, but it's well ahead of whatever's in second place.

December 19, 1979.

People around the country have come up with various ways to keep the hostages in mind.

Some wear armbands, some tie ribbons on the old oak tree, or any other tree available.

Some hold prayer meetings, some fly the flag—and some merely count the days.

I suppose the important thing is that we keep them in mind, and however we choose to do that, if it works, is the proper way.

January 2, 1980.
I am a bit confused....

For the past two months the United States has been brought more or less to a halt through the actions of a mob.

A mob, like all mobs, that blusters, and boasts, and cares nothing at all for reason or legality.

And further, in the past few days, we've seen a new development—that being the Soviet Union's invasion of Afghanistan.

Oh, they say it's all very democratic; but word has it that most of the votes are being cast by means of armed force.

I'm fairly clear on those facts.

What I'm confused about is why we haven't heard from Jane Fonda?

January 14, 1980.
The news from Iran is likely to be second or third hand and even more confusing in coming days.

The revolutionary council which heads up the chaos in Iran has decreed that all American reporters must leave.

They're biased—the American reporters—and so Iran is kicking them out.

It seems they failed to notice the difference in the system employed by the Shah and the new system put into effect by the Ayatollah and his mob.

You see, under the Shah, one group ruled the other group by repression and murder; under the Ayatollah, it's just the other way around.

February 13, 1980.
It was a real pleasure to read the letters to the editor in the Washington *Post* today.

They were mainly from Canadians, Canadians who appreciate the fact that there has been an outpouring of gratitude from this country toward theirs for their rescue of six of our diplomats from Iran.

But one was a special pleasure.

It noted that America has been in the habit of rescuing people and countries for a long time, and that "Thank You USA" signs have been notable by their absence.

Another noted that he would like to call himself a Canadian and an American, and would we mind if he did that.

I suspect that we don't mind at all.

April 9, 1980.

The other day an American State Department official was trying to explain to Iran's charge d'affaires, Ali Agha, that he was no longer welcome in the United States.

In so doing, the official directed at Mr. Agha and his aide an old American phrase that roughly translates into several meanings, depending on the context.

Two rather simple four-letter words that are sometimes used on the fringes of polite society to describe one's feeling of disbelief, consternation, disagreement, feelings that one is being lied to, and express a greater scope of meaning than "horsefeathers" which is as close as I can get on television.

It is a phrase that could best be described in diplomatic terms as candid.

In this case the State Department official was trying to explain the worth of the Iranian stand on the matters that divide our two countries.

And with two simple words, he hit the nail right on the head.

April 11, 1980.

It seems our allies in western Europe and Japan as well have been able to solidly get together on one issue: that being that Iran is the United States' problem.

Japan was pretty straightforward about it; the word from Tokyo was that Japan just can't join in economic sanctions against Iran.

The foreign ministers of the European Community were a little more vague.

They met and decided they can't help right now.

One spokesman who asked, understandably, not to be identified, came out of the meeting and ventured the opinion that America should not consider this rejection a slap in the face. After all, he said, Europe might change its mind later on.

Neville Chamberlain couldn't have put it any better.

May 5, 1980.
I received a letter from a young lady in Virginia Beach this morning who was quite upset with me—said she had just watched me for the last time.

It seems she felt that my use of the word animals to describe the militants holding the American hostages was uncalled for, and a racist remark, and who did I think I was anyway.

Well, the broadcast she had reference to was one in which I made reference to the obscenely ghoulish behavior of the Ayatollah Kalkhali and the militants when they put on their sideshow with the bodies of some heroic Americans.

I must admit, I did call them animals and that was unfair.

I apologize to all animals and friends of animals.

May 7, 1980.
Driving back from dinner tonight, I listened to a radio talk show where listener and host were kicking around an idea I've heard several times lately.

That being, if we could get the networks to stop carrying news from Iran, the terrorists and Khomeini would tire of the game and free the hostages.

For those in touch with history, I need hardly point out that that's precisely the way the world dealt with the menace of Adolf Hitler.

It ignored him in the twenties and expected him to go away.

We all know how well that worked.

Nosir, the militant mob and the fanatic who leads them are not a pleasant bunch, and hearing and seeing their attempts to make unacceptable behaviour acceptable is painful.

So is cancer....

And pretending that it isn't there, with a cancer or an enemy, is the surest road to defeat.

May 21, 1980.
It was two hundred days ago that those Iranian militants took the American Embassy in Teheran, and somewhat less than that since the Soviet Union invaded the nation of Afghanistan, at the invitation of a puppet they had put in office.

We were indignant at both events, most of us, and we remain indignant, most of us.

But, judging from the response among our allies and sportsmen abroad to suggestions of sanctions and Olympic boycotts, we are in the minority.

The excuse—America's foreign policy takes too many turns.

Well sir, maybe I'm old-fashioned but turning one's back on a proven friend simply because that friend may be big and clumsy is a shabby way to behave.

There's still the matter of right and wrong to consider, and in these two cases we may be clumsy, but we are right.

June 10, 1980.

According to Teheran Radio, which the other day called him the vilest of agents, Ramsey Clark is now a true patriot of America and President Carter had better not punish him for his trip to Iran to attend the Crimes of America Conference.

Anyway, Iran's opinion of Ramsey Clark is apparently subject to change from time to time.

The mystery here is Clark's opinion of Iran and the chaos that passes for a government there.

Ramsey Clark is a lawyer.

Just now he's pleading the case for a government that is systematically persecuting Jews and members of the Bahai faith, and one that denies defense counsel to defendants on trial and takes its cue on international law and diplomacy from such notable leaders of the past as Attila the Hun and the Barbary Pirates.

And he wants us...to apologize to them.

June 27, 1980.

The Ayatollah Khomeini took his government to task today.

He warned that there might well be a political upheaval in Iran if Bani Sadr's government doesn't get off its duff and do something.

He called the government bureaucracies ineffective and evil, noting that the country faces turmoil on every hand, a devastated economy and continued violence between rival political factions.

Horror of horrors, some government offices still haven't

scraped the insignia of the Shah's regime off their doors. Doesn't it all just break your heart?

August 6, 1980.
    I talked to a number of people today who were uniformly angry about the release of those pro-Khomeini Iranians who were arrested for rioting in Washington last week.
    I don't like it either.
    After all, they are, by their own admission enemies of our system, advocates of a system that would happily destroy us, one that proves daily that it has no regard for human rights, dignity, due process, truth, or common decency.
    And here they enjoy the protection of the law while their own country's government pursues a policy of terrorism.
    It's infuriating.
    It's also one of the things that makes our system worth whatever trouble it takes to preserve it.
    All their efforts to prove our system wrong merely demonstrate how very right it is.
    As for theirs, we won't have to destroy it, they're doing that job very well.

January 22, 1981.
    The great national debate has started. During the day yesterday, last night, and all day today we've been hearing compelling reasons why the United States should now refuse to honor any elements of the hostage agreement with Iran that have not already been completed.
    There are arguments, just as reasonable, that we should honor those agreements, especially if doing so is in our national interest.
    Personally, I am inclined to agree with those who would let Iran whistle for anything they haven't already got in their hot little hands, but I could be wrong about that.
    So, on the chance that the hard line might be the wrong line, a brief waiting period to sort things out might be in order.
    Just a little pause to assure us that all details have been duly weighed and considered....
    ...four hundred forty-four days should be about right.

January 26, 1981.
    I wonder if the fifty-two citizens who finally came home to America yesterday will recognize it as the same country

they left so long ago.

Fourteen months, of course, is an eternity if you're unjustly held prisoner, or if you're a member of the hostage's family, or even if you're just a fellow citizen, worried about them.

But, in the life of a nation, fourteen months is a very short time. It ordinarily takes some years to see major changes take place.

When the hostages left home we were still caught up in that post Vietnam syndrome where making a fuss over the flag or taking patriotism seriously were viewed as something at least slightly suspect, sometimes as something very suspect.

Nowadays you'll see the signs and symbols of a proud nation and a proud people just about anywhere you look. And nobody seems to be attaching labels lately.

Isn't it nice?

Don't you hope it lasts?

CHAPTER 7

Great events shape history of course, eveybody knows that. But so do little ones.

When Mrs. O'Leary's cow kicked over the lantern in O'Leary's barn, it caused O'Leary's barn to burn down. That was, on a world scale, a small event had O'Leary's barn not ignited the fire that destroyed Chicago.

From time to time I pass on stories that seem insignificant.

I just can't take the chance that another O'Leary's cow may be in there somewhere.

As Kitty Kallen used to sing to us in the fifties....

LITTLE THINGS MEAN A LOT

July 17, 1979.

I've noticed a certain phenomenon over the past few summers and I'm sure it's one that a psychiatrist could have some fun with. But for me it's just an annoyance.

That is that the temperature and the relative humidity of summer weather have a direct and definite effect on my feelings toward the necktie.

In the winter when a necktie is no more than a useless vanity, I dislike neckties; but I do not actively hate them.

But in the summer when the necktie becomes the most efficient heat and moisture retainer known to man, my dislike turns to cold and calculating hatred.

I do, however, continue to wear neckties—and for a good and valid reason.

My boss, you see, loves neckties. In his opinion, they look especially nice on working anchormen.

Non-working anchormen may wear anything they like.

November 29, 1979.

It's one of those things that happens a lot, but we rarely hear about it.

A man I know in the Coast Guard called today and told me how he and his wife were shopping last night, and in the confusion of loading their purchases in the car, the wife's purse was left on the ground in the parking lot, its absence unnoticed until they got home.

In the purse, the family's credit cards, cash, identification, all those things wives carry and husbands give wives to carry.

In short...a calamity.

But, an honest man found that purse, took it to a nearby store. The store called my friend, and everything got back like it was supposed to be.

My friend wanted to thank the honest man involved, but he didn't leave his name.

I suspect that such things happen all the time, but hardly anybody ever calls the police to report a case of honesty.

It pleases me to be able to report this one.

December 10, 1979.

And before we go, just an item or so that might otherwise be missed in the welter of events.

RCA, the communications company, launched a new communications satellite last Thursday, and they've been trying to find it ever since.

Phoenix, Arizona, the clean air city, is under smog alert.

In Atlanta, J. K. Ramey has a sign to warn visitors about Atlanta's criminal element—a bill board, right on top of his tire store. It's proclaimed the message for days now that you have to be extremely cautious in Atlanta.

Ramey knows whereof he speaks; his store was robbed again last Saturday.

And, the Reverend Joe McAfee, a former burglar, recently had this tip for those who wish to avoid being victimized by those who still work his former trade.

Don't hide your jewels in the freezer.

With the price of meat nowadays, that's the first place a good burglar looks.

December 12, 1979.

Each day the Associated Press sends us a note on the day, listing some of the important historic events that occurred on this date, some of the birthdays of important or famous persons, and so on.

And today's note, I thought, was especially interesting in that it shows how small events can have great meaning.

In 1792, the great composer Franz Joseph Haydn was supporting himself by giving music lessons.

On December 12th that year he took a new student; the

price: nineteen cents a lesson. The student's name was Ludwig van Beethoven.

January 29, 1980.
I'm afraid there's going to be trouble.
The *Times* of London, one of the world's most respected newspapers, has abolished a word.
The *Times* puts it this way; it's artificial, ugly and silly, it means nothing, and besides it's rotten grammar.
The *Times* goes on to describe the word in question as a faddish middle class plaything, one of the excesses of a revolution, and should be junked.
The word in question: Ms.
Ms. is out, as far as *The Times* is concerned, except when they want to use it as the abbreviation for manuscript.
It's hard to argue with *The Times* of London's grammar. Their sense of timing, however, is quite another question.
There's going to be trouble.

February 28, 1980.
I was fascinated to learn today, through the Washington *Post,* that last Thursday was Zip Code Day in Vienna, Virginia.
The reason it was Zip Code Day was because Vienna's zip code, with a couple of slashes added, translates out to the date, February 2, '80.
In Vienna, that's as good a reason as any to have a special day: And, if you're going to have a special day, naturally, a parade is in order.
So, the good folks of Vienna got the high school band, a mob of politicians, some jeeps from the post office, and Joe Theismann from the Redskins, and had a parade.
Just to guarantee a crowd, they held the parade during rush hour. Several speeches were made, but I liked Joe Theismann's the best.
He made the point. "Very few places in the world have the zip code we do—and we should be honored by that."
Think about that ....

March 26, 1980.
I've always been a sucker for hero stories, and when the hero happens to be a dog, even better.
Over in Carroll County last weekend, a three-year-old

boy wandered away from home, and quite naturally, a search was launched.

The people involved couldn't find the youngster, so State trooper Garry Boyette and his tracking dog Trace were called in.

It took some time, but Trace stayed on the job, and finally found the youngster a mile from home, wading in a creek, but safe and sound.

So, it's reasonable to suppose now that the dog Trace is referred to as Mister Trace, keener than most persons.

I forgot to mention—I'm also a sucker for puns.

March 28, 1980.

If you count sheep in order to fall asleep at night, you might be interested in the results of a scientific study I've recently run across.

It's not the green pastures and serene animals that do the trick.

A research team at Harvard has discovered that visualizing sheep prevents the brain's right hemisphere from processing anxiety-provoking imagery, while counting them keeps the left hemisphere from straying into problematic auditory and verbal thought.

I think I understand that, some of it; and if I do, it follows that we'd be as well off counting whales.

It's interesting to know that sheep counting has value for scientific reasons, but it sure takes the charm out of it.

April 23, 1980.

Here's a report from Roanoke that has a moral in it somewhere.

This rather portly fellow's car stalled, and that was bad. But it was at the top of a hill, and that was good.

So, he and another fellow started to push the car to get it started, the driver reaching in the window to steer. Well, once the car was rolling well the driver decided to get in.

That's when he discovered that the door was locked. So, he decided to crawl into the car, which was moving pretty smartly by this time, through the window.

That's when he discovered that he was wider than the window.

So, the car continued down the hill with the steering end of the driver inside where it belonged, and the braking end—

in this case the most essential end—waving gaily in the breeze.

Three blocks and twenty-five-hundred dollars in property damages later, the car finally stopped, and thankfully, no one was hurt.

That is if you don't count wounded dignity as an injury.

I don't exactly know what the moral is, but I'm sure there is one.

June 24, 1980.

I'll never forgive myself for missing Mike and Kyrie Dimmagio's wedding in Berwyn, Illinois.

I don't know them, but it has to be the social event of the season in many respects.

For instance, the reception at the Elks Club Hall attracted not only two hundred guests—who proceeded to choose sides in a brawl—but twelve arrests, made by a total of forty-five officers; a hole in one wall made either by a champagne bottle, or a fist; and a two hundred-fifty-dollar wedding cake which nobody ate, but which a lot of people threw at each other.

But, apparently Kyrie was listening to that part about for better or for worse. She left with Michael on a honeymoon, slightly delayed because she had to bail him out of the Berwyn jail first.

The report I saw didn't say what the bride's mother wore; but I sorta suspect she wished she'd worn a football helmet.

July 28, 1980.

Having grown up in an era when there were very few big fancy car washes around, I have remained fairly ignorant of how they operate.

It does please me that they are doing well, but I'm afraid car washes and I will never be great friends. I've used three in my lifetime, and each time it was a traumatic experience.

The first one ate two perfectly serviceable side mounted mirrors.

The second demonstrated the wisdom of double-checking a window you're sure you remember having rolled up.

And the third showed me that bumpers on modern cars are not always as securely attached as one might hope.

Anyway, I remain convinced that the most reliable mechanism for washing a car is a bucket of soapy water, a garden hose, and an eleven-year-old who needs money for roller skates.

September 3, 1980.
I've been hearing all my life, and you probably have too, that too much of a good thing can kill you.
Well, add another health hazard to the list.
If you don't, the Food and Drug Administration probably will now that Theodore Kemper and Rosalynn Wallach Bologh have finished their research.
They say it's healthy to do this the first time and even a second and third time, perhaps over the course of a lifetime. But, do it too often, and you may turn up with nervous disorders, digestive problems, headaches, rashes and severe itching.
What is it you ask?
Falling in love.
I guess the old poem will have to be amended.
It's better to have loved and lost—in moderation—than never to have loved at all.

September 8, 1980.
I always enjoy those little features on the wire and in the papers that mention the important birthdays and historical events that took place on this day. It's always easy to use hindsight to bear and note how this or that changed history.
It was on this day in 1974, for instance, that President Ford pardoned Richard Nixon.
Back in 1935, Huey Long was assassinated.
Back in 1664, Peter Stuyvesant surrendered New Amsterdam to the British, who chose to call it New York.
But the event I would choose that seems to me to have had more effect on the way we live than any of the above happened fifty years ago today...and involved a man named Richard Drew.
Richard Drew wasn't a statesman, or a politician and as far as I know, never won any wars or discovered any countries.
He did, however, invent Scotch tape.

September 9, 1980.
A janitor out in Chicago took an unusual approach to the art of extermination.

It seems his building was plagued with rats.

It seems he had also heard somewhere that rats do not like snakes.

So, he went out and rounded up about fifty non-poisonous garter snakes, and set them loose in the building.

What he had neglected to research, however, was the fact that some people feel almost as strongly about snakes, even harmless snakes, as they do about rats.

The tenants left, according to reports, with great speed, and so did the janitor. Nobody has seen him lately and the story doesn't even give his name.

We're pretty sure it wasn't Otto the Orkin Man.

September 12, 1980.

While we're on the subject of birthdays, I guess it's probably no news, by this time of day, that today is the 100th anniversary of the birth of H. L. Mencken.

Most of us who write for a living have noticed; and most of us have wished that we might be able to do what Mencken did so well—that is, comment on the world, where it's been and where it's likely to go, and with enough wit and humor to make the news bearable.

H. L. Mencken was a hard man to like, and he intended to be; and he brought a great deal of artistic energy to the business of making us see ourselves as others see us.

I can read Mencken and find something I wish I'd written in almost every line. But I think my favorite was his definition of conscience.

Conscience, he said, is the inner voice that warns us somebody may be looking.

November 7, 1980.

Some unidentified troublemaker brought a box of jelly doughnuts into the Thirteen newsroom today, and I was faced with an old problem.

I don't eat jelly donuts.

I like jelly donuts.

In fact, I'm crazy about jelly donuts.

But I don't eat them because no matter how carefully I plan my attack on a jelly donut, at least half of the jelly winds up on my tie.

Napkins don't help; bibs, knives and forks don't help; no matter how I eat a jelly donut, I wind up wearing most of the jelly, and a not inconsiderable portion of the sugar glaze they're always equipped with.

So, I avoided those delightful booby traps of the pastry world, and watched with glee when my producer chose one of the fattest of the lot.

Justice, I thought, it's going to happen to somebody else.

But it didn't.

He consumed it to the last bite without staining even one fingertip.

I consider that, at the very least, unkind.

May 5, 1981.

If you were wondering where I was yesterday when I should have been here, I'll tell you.

In fact, I'll tell you whether you were wondering or not.

For one thing, it was moving day at the Kincaids'. For another, I had a dental appointment.

I don't know about you, but these are both activities that I look forward to with less than enthusiasm. But my dentist is a gentle man, and he brought me through so painlessly that I hardly screamed at all.

And that bite on his hand will probably heal in no time.

And the movers got everything out of one apartment and into another without breaking or losing a thing. I would have helped, but I have this old back problem that always crops up when I'm in the presence of heavy lifting.

I probably would have made it through the day okay if I hadn't decided to be useful and run a quality control check on the icemaker in the new apartment. I did this while I unpacked and rearranged the bar.

I must have overworked or something.

This morning I was in poor health, in every category, except hearing. My hearing had actually improved; it was the first thing I noticed when the birds started shouting.

I'll say this as quietly as I can....

Join us again at eleven...and stay tuned for ABC World News Tonight.

May 25, 1981.

As I announced earlier this evening, the registration of a temperature above ninety degrees has the same effect on me every year.

Ordinarily, in cool weather, I regard the necktie as a mere

nuisance, something to be endured. But, when it gets hot and sticky, I remember all of a sudden that the necktie is my enemy, a thing to dread.

It is, after all, a folly, a caprice dreamed up and thrust on the western world by one of the French kings named Louis. I believe it was Louis the Fourteenth; but it could have been the Sixteenth, and it doesn't really matter.

Anyway, this particular Louis had some Croatian mercenaries working for him, and when they weren't off fighting a war, they just laid around the palace.

They wore long scarves tied around their necks, probably because the palace didn't have central heating, and Louis thought they were cute. And when a king thinks something is cute, all sorts of people rush right out to buy one.

This particular Louis, if I recall, also had a prejudice against taking baths.

I can remember a time in my life when I could have agreed with him on that, but my mother had other ideas.

I just wish Louis' mercenaries had worn T-shirts.

June 29, 1981.

I was pretty hard put to find something to comment on today.

As for this day in history, and what significant event might have occurred on this date, all I could come up with was the information that it was on this day in 1925 that the first patent was approved for a frosted lightbulb.

It looked for a while like we might have a real story out in Arizona.

A fellow out there was supposed to lead his flock on a bodily ascension into heaven; but even though they quit their jobs for the occasion it seems everybody is still solidly on the ground near Tucson.

Over in West Germany a couple of Polish bicycle racers have turned up—in Hannover. The race was in Baden, seems they overshot the finish line a bit. I guess they're so embarrassed they don't want to face anybody back home; they've applied for political asylum.

And in Iran, the Ayatollah's folks are showing their skill at criminology. They know for certain that it was the United States behind that explosion last night.

As for the whereabouts of their recent president, Bani Sadr—well, that's another matter.

July 28, 1981.
I've neglected lately to keep you up to date on major holidays coming up.
Tomorrow, of course, there's the wedding of Prince Charles and Lady Diana; and it will be a festive occasion, no doubt. When it comes to pageantry our mother country does the job properly, no question about it.
But in the frenzy around the nuptials, we almost forgot that tomorrow is also Asphalt Road Day. That's right. It was on July 29, 1870 that the first asphalt road was constructed in Newark, New Jersey. I've been to Newark, and I'm sure that I've driven on that very road.
But you don't have to go to Newark; we have some asphalt roads right here in Tidewater that appear to have been contructed one hundred and eleven years ago, and one can get the same sense of history without even leaving town.
It's my belief, though I can't prove it, that the hundred eleventh anniversary of the first pothole in an asphalt road should probably be celebrated sometime next week.
It would be a more significant anniversary; after all, when was the last time you remarked on an asphalt road.
Potholes, on the other hand, get our attention and inspire some of our more colorful language.

September 9, 1981.
I thought I'd fill these last moments tonight with some news items you might not otherwise know about.
For instance, as a service to runners with hay fever, this is the time of year when ragweed begins to have an effect; we suggest an antihistamine for the hay fever, a psychiatrist for the urge to run.
From London comes news that Venkat Ali went to sleep while waiting for a plane to Pakistan. While he slept, somebody stole his false teeth.
If you were planning to go to the Miss America pageant especially to hear Miss North Dakota sing, don't. She has laryngitis and will have to recite instead.
For our hypochondriac fans, good news. There are several new diseases you might not have suffered just yet; among them, Casino Feet, caused by standing too long while risking the rent money; Disco Neuropathy, caused by skating too long to disco music while wearing tight-fitting roller skates; and, Golfer's Grief, a severe depression brought on by

weekend rainstorms.
 We understand this can also affect members of the medical profession on rainy Wednesday afternoons.

JIM KINCAID

HAS FLOWN WITH MEMBERS OF THE
UNITED STATES AIR FORCE IN AERIAL COMBAT OVER THE REPUBLIC OF VIETNAM

DATE 29 JULY 1970

TYPE ACFT A-37

F.A.C. REPORT: BUNKER COMPLEX DESTROYED

PILOT 1ST LT. DEE W. FRIESEN

TARGET 18 MILES WEST OF TAY NINH IN BINH DUONG PROVINCE

Dee W. Friesen 1st Lt USAF

A memento of Viet Nam.

Viet Nam, 1969.

Viet Nam, 1970.

A Buddhist
temple in Vientiane,
Laos, 1969.

Two of the hundreds
of press cards I collected
over three decades.

Peter Jennings and I interviewing Jimmy Hoffa.

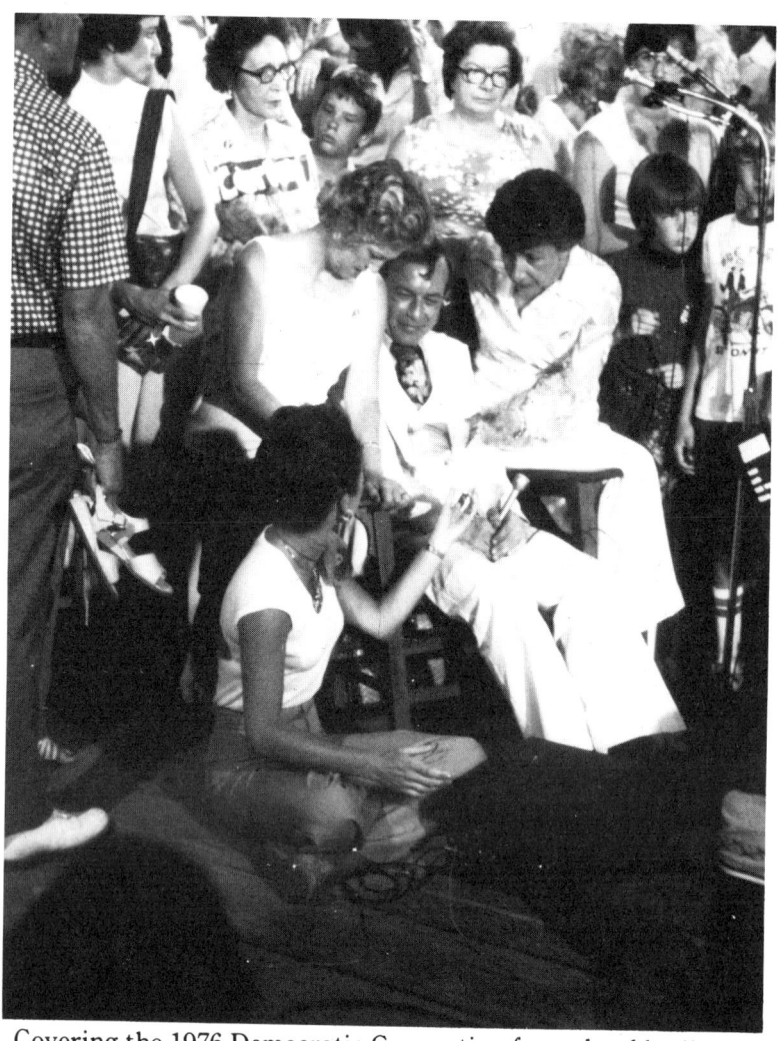

Covering the 1976 Democratic Convention from the old railroad station in Plains, Georgia.

Elam.

Louise Foreman's restored cabin at Elam.

The Foreman cabin, long view.

Battered by the years, but still "hanging in."

One of Theo Wildanger's (my father-in-law) many conceptions of Elam.

An oil in progress by Theo Wildanger.

Murphy and his bosom buddy Critter, who believes he's also an Irish Setter.

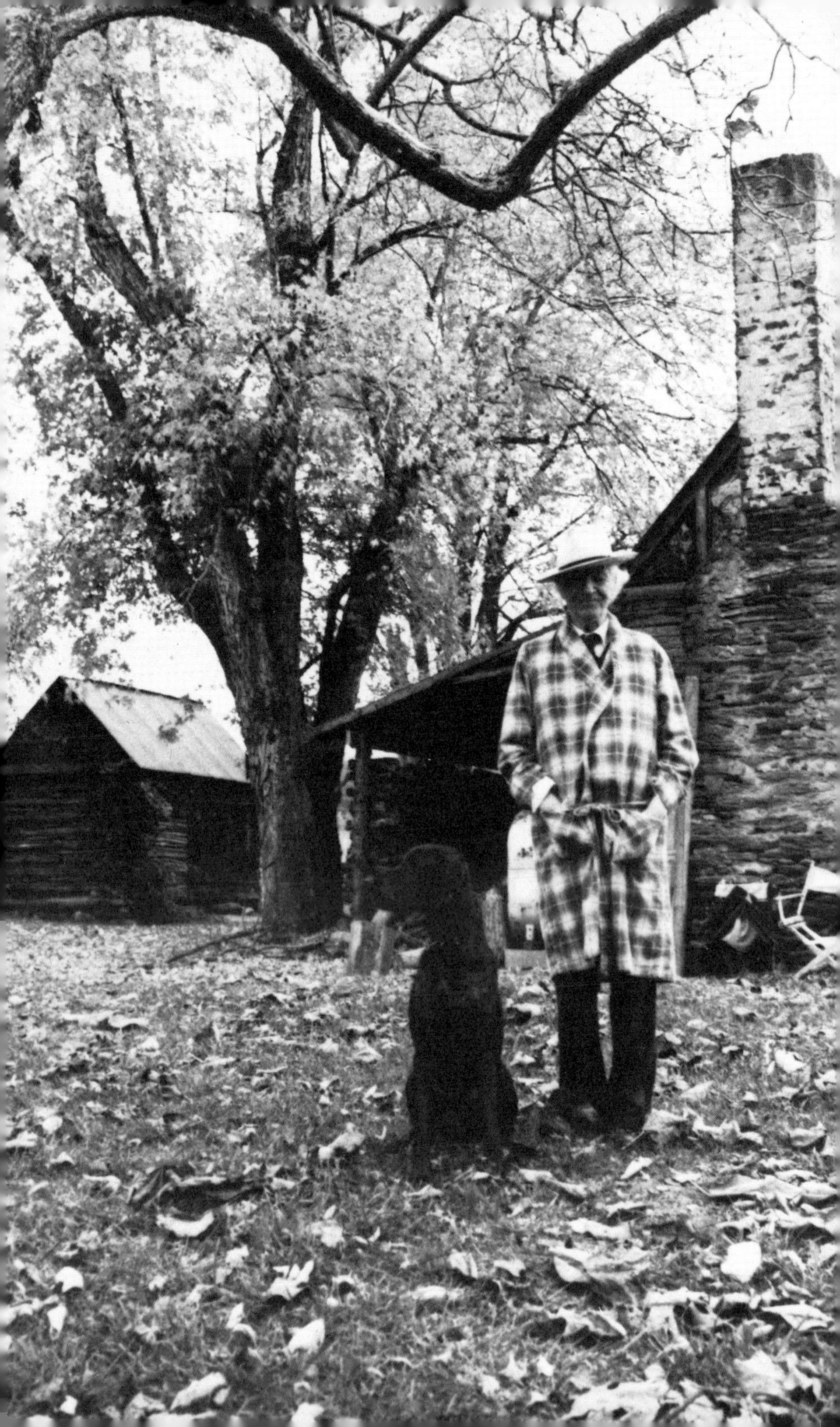

Theo and Murphy.

Stranger taking the sun.

Stranger and Fifi heading for a backdoor handout.

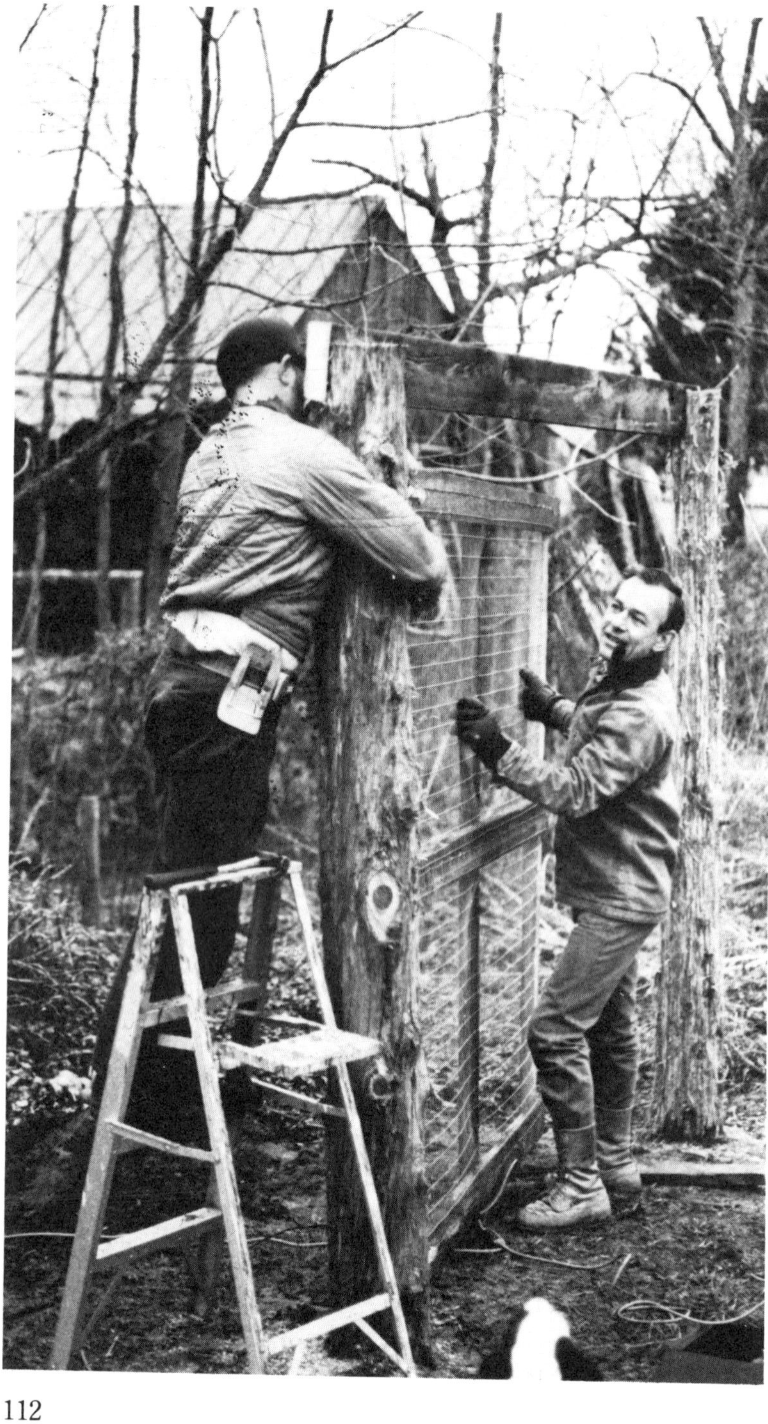

Kids, dogs, and country music... weekends are like that at Elam.

Luther Lewis and I, hanging an allegedly rabbit-proof gate.

Murphy in a quiet moment.

A family portrait, with wife Catherine, daughter Carolyn, Critter, and, oh yes, Murphy on the right.

114

CHAPTER 8

Some reporters specialize. They find early on that they have a knack for science or policitics or economics or whatever, and that's what they write about.

I noticed some time back that I never got around to doing that.

I discussed it with the boss, and said I guessed I'm just sort of a reporter-at-large.

He said he thought of me as being not so much at large as....

AT RANDOM

November 12, 1979.

I have managed, not to quit smoking, but to wean myself from cigarettes to what many consider a less harmful form of smoking.

I smoke a pipe and though I have always smoked a pipe to some extent, I now smoke a pipe to the exclusion of all other forms of smoking.

I would like to do more but I cannot; and I know that the twenty-four-hour Great American Smokeout will be, for me, an exercise in guilt.

My colleagues will parade their smokeless selves by my desk and shake their heads sadly at my degradation; and I will feel guilty—from behind a cloud of smoke.

I hate to do it but I will have to bring to bear the ultimate weapon at my command: I plan to fix each one with an icy stare and ask: "When was the last time you wrote to your mother?"

November 28, 1979.

According to reports that have been circulating all week, there's a photographer from *Playboy* Magazine in Tidewater on a recruiting mission; that being, to recruit women in uniform.

I guess that's misleading. The fellow from *Playboy* is looking for women who might otherwise be in uniform if they were not auditioning for an appearance in the pages of *Playboy* magazine.

We have been unable to get a clear statement of policy

115

from the military as to just how out of uniform one has to be to incur the wrath of the brass. But, as I understand it, the policy of *Playboy* would dictate that the women in question be extremely out of uniform.

I wouldn't know for sure, of course. I only read the articles.

January 14, 1980.

Tomorrow night at this hour I will be on a very special assignment, that being to make the introduction when Howard K. Smith speaks to the Norfolk Forum.

To give you an idea of what such an assignment means to me, I should point out that he's the only celebrity from whom I have ever requested an autograph.

He'll be speaking on the challenges facing this country. And I plan to do as I've done in the past, and plagiarize his thoughts shamelessly.

I don't think he'll tell us to worry any less about our country, but perhaps how to worry more efficiently.

January 16, 1980.

I promised on Monday that I would plagiarize shamelessly from Howard K. Smith's lecture of last night at Chrysler Hall. And one of his descriptions of the Soviet attitude toward detente seems just the right size to steal.

Howard told of a tour he made of the Moscow zoo once with a Russian colleague. The Russian wanted to show him a special symbol of how his country sees detente. So he took Howard to a cage where there was a huge and ferocious Russian bear; and there, in the same cage, a lamb, sleeping peacefully.

That, said the Russian, is detente.

Wonderful, said Howard, and you mean to tell me that it works?

Certainly it works, said the Russian. Of course, we have to have replace the lamb every morning.

January 28, 1980.

The debate seems to have started.

Whether to register young people for the draft, as we did before in times of trouble, and whether those registered should be men only, or men and women.

The arguments for and against are the same ones we

heard the last time the draft was in force, and they're good arguments mostly.

To me, the most telling argument against the draft is the theory that it's always the old and wealthy telling the young and poor to preserve the peace, or win the conflict.

And the most telling argument for it is the theory that the draft is necessary to maintain a system that provides one of the better chances on this planet for the young and poor to get to be old and wealthy.

February 12, 1980.

I have in my lifetime collected many things, stamps, coins and matchbook covers, but never with any degree of success.

I can report, however, that I have, till now, collected each and every variety of flu on this planet, and am sure, once it's available in this area, that I will have Singapore flu as well.

I am equally sure that I will not have to seek out Singapore flu. It will, like every other strain of flu, find me no matter where I hide.

So, if I turn up missing one night soon, you'll know it's nothing serious; they're just test marketing Singapore flu in Tidewater.

February 28, 1980.

If you're the sort who likes to plan ahead, and your name is Cranz—spelled C-R-A-N-Z—Have I got a deal for you.

It's a 550-pound marble tombstone, never used, good as new.

You'll have to get in touch with Art Cranz of Mays Landing, New Jersey. Seems Cranz had a close relative who thought she was about to cash in on account of a serious illness; so he ordered up a tombstone.

Well, as luck would have it, the lady got well.

So Cranz ran an ad, a simple ad.

"Monument Tombstone For Sale...Didn't Die...Don't Need It."

March 6, 1980.

I read Cammy Sessa's *Virginian-Pilot* review of Charlotte Ford's new book on modern manners today; I was delighted to know that for $14.95, we'll be able to *learn* how to behave ourselves properly again.

Cammy points out that the 509-page book Ms. Ford has

117

written explains just about everything we need to know except why we should regard Ms. Ford as an authority on etiquette.

To me, the most fascinating revelation in the Ford book is the news that it's all right to eat an artichoke with one's fingers.

That's just going to thrill artichoke lovers to pieces.

It will also occur to some of them, who consider the matter carefully, that it's physically impossible to eat an artichoke any other way.

April 2, 1980

I've been thinking that the worst thing that could happen to me this year would be an income tax audit.

I didn't cheat on my taxes, I just have this irrational fear of authority. Anyway, the census forms have come along to complicate my life even further. I got two copies, one at the farm, at Elam, the other at the apartment, where I live during the week.

My problem is this: If I fill out one or the other, I'm technically accurate, but liable to fine for failure to answer one of the forms. If I fill out both, the country will appear to have four extra persons, and it would be all my fault.

I'm sure it will all work out; but by the time I get over this crisis it'll be time to try to remember if you set the clock back an hour or forward an hour to compensate for Daylight Saving Time.

It's just one darn thing after another.

April 14, 1980.

There's a song that's been around for a few years that goes, in part, "rainy days and Mondays always get me down...."

Well, they don't always get me down, but today I have to admit defeat. Over the weekend I found several new groundhog burrows near my garden.

My grass was too wet to mow this week, and it'll be too high to mow next week.

Rain on a tin roof always lulls me off to sleep, except for last night.

I've got a backache that even arthritis strength pain formula won't handle.

And tomorrow is income tax deadline.

All that and Monday, too—who wouldn't feel rotten.
I'll probably be more cheerful at eleven, but I wouldn't bet on it.

April 21, 1980.
This, in case you haven't been watching the calendar, is the beginning of National Secretaries Week.

During the week, it's hoped that bosses throughout the land will take the time to appreciate the secretaries of the land; that they, by the technical, formal, and literate definition, should be considered more than just employees.

They are, after all, the keepers of order in a disorderly world.

They are managers of time in a world where time is money in the truest sense of the word.

It might be a good week to try a revolutionary experiment and give that secretary of yours a day or two off without a replacement, temporary or otherwise.

My guess is that making your own coffee will be the least of your problems.

May 9, 1980.
I had the very distinct honor early this afternoon to attend a groundbreaking in Virginia Beach.

The Volunteers of America were turning the first shovelfuls of earth for what will be, by the first of next year, a home for mentally retarded adults.

Not a homelike atmosphere, mind you, but a home; the sort of place where you can hang pictures, sit in your own chair, sleep in your own bed, and help with the dishes.

Two dozen or so of us gathered on the grounds of Good Samaritan Church. There were some short and modest speeches and many months of planning and work started becoming a reality.

It occurred to me, coming away from it all, that one of the last luxuries Americans ever think about giving up, even in times of economic troubles, is that of helping those who need our help.

June 2, 1980.
Something happened at a recent meeting of the Tennessee Valley Authority that illustrates one of the problems the people of this country have with the people who run their government.

It seems they were having a meeting to explain to some local folks the effect of a new power plant. TVA chairman David Freeman talked about solar conservation interfaces and about cogeneration capacity. When a local farmer asked him about the possibility that some of the concrete blocks in his house might be slightly radioactive, Freeman told the man not to worry, that the study universe was too small.

The man wasn't entirely satisfied, I guess. Says he, "I'm not asking you about the whole darn universe, I just want to know about my house."

Even a board chairman of TVA should be able to understand that.

June 9, 1980.

Plagiarism, as any English student knows, is the copying of someone else's writing, and claiming of it as one's own; and it's a terrible crime among writers.

So, I've always practiced a policy of giving credit when I swipe someone else's lines, or thoughts, especially if there's a chance I'll be caught at it.

But here's one for the book.

Out in Eugene, Oregon, the professors of English at the University of Oregon published a handbook for students, one that includes a section on plagiarism.

It's an elegant passage and details the enormity of this literary crime. And it was stolen, word for word, from the Stanford University handbook.

June 23, 1980.

After a wonderful week of vacation on the farm at Elam, I must express thanks to Jane Gardner for filling in for me while I withdrew from the news world.

That is to say that I made a point of not keeping up with what's going on, right up to the very last day of my vacation.

I did peek at a newspaper occasionally to determine what day it was and kept an eye and an ear out for rain, which we badly need here and at Elam.

But, imagine my surprise when I finally got in touch again late yesterday and found America on the brink of total collapse.

Precisely where it's been for the past two hundred and four years.

July 2, 1980.
   Back in my youth, it came to pass that my government found itself unable to continue to sustain democracy without my help; and I, along with a number of friends, submitted to the draft.
   So I was able to understand the concerns, a few days back, of a young man who told a congressional committee that registration for the draft, *registration* mind you, would constitute an invasion of his privacy.
   It is inconvenient, and certainly not pleasant, to have one's government know where to find one in the event one is needed.
   In fact, millions of Americans can tell you that it's not unknown for the government to call on one for some years of service.
   I did want to ask the young fellow, however, one question.
   That being, how he thought he came by that right of privacy in the first place?

September 16, 1980.
   When Joe Foulkes makes his speech on hurricanes tonight before the assembled Civil Defense people, he'll be calling on the science of meteorology, a calling he's very good at and conversant with... and I think I just dangled a couple of participles.
   Anyway, as good as Joe is at the business of predicting what the weather will do, and why it will do it, you may have noticed that he hasn't come up with any winter information here in this last week of summer.
   I hate to have to cover for Joe, but he just hates to break bad news. It will, in fact, be an early winter this year and a severe one.
   Much as I hate to be the bearer of bad tidings, facts is facts.
   At Elam this weekend I saw two woolly bear caterpillars. They were very fuzzy, and very dark brown.

September 22, 1980.
   I'm always rushing the season.
   Fall, of course, is the flu and cold season; But I just couldn't wait, and about the middle of last week I came down with one of those things that have been going around.

And came down is the right word.

A cold or a viral infection can reduce me to a state of helplessness and misery beyond imagination. My wife, on the other hand, has to be sure to mention it when she has a cold, or I'm likely not to notice. She carries it off with such dignity, such nonchalance, such strength.

Then there's Judith Baroody and Jane Gardner. They do this program in my absence maddeningly well.

Wonder drugs, as we all know, have no effect on a cold. Pride, on the other hand, has remarkable healing powers.

September 23, 1980.

In my growing up years I have always loved two types of music above all others, grand opera on the one hand, especially Italian opera, and hillbilly music. Nowadays they call it country, but down in Arkansas we called it hillbilly.

I always considered that an odd combination, and was slightly ashamed of it, and never talked about it openly until recently.

But then recently, Mister Pavarotti appeared jointly with Dolly Parton; and it hit me....

Italian opera and hillbilly music are about the same things. Cheating lovers, broken hearts, being homesick ...misunderstood, drinking too much, and not knowing where your next meal's coming from.

So, I can come out of the closet now and admit it openly and proudly that my two favorite singers are Enrico Caruso and Willie Nelson.

November 10, 1980.

This law shop thing has all sorts of possibilities.

America has always been the one place in the world where an idea could catch on, especially a good idea; and what with the price of everything else going up, it's got to be a good idea to set up shop and offer the good article at an affordable price.

I'm going to keep an eye on the law shop; and if it works out, I plan to open a philosophy shop. For a dollar or so I could deliver a political philosophy.

Couldn't charge much more than that for one, because political philosophies don't last too long.

Look at those from the sixties, for example, they're all worn out and most of them cost a good deal more than a dollar.

I think the country is ready for a chain of fast philosophy shoppes.
Instead of golden arches we could use an ivory tower.

November 13, 1980.
With the approach of the Voyager to Saturn in recent days, the old debate is on again.
What good is it? Don't we have enough problems on Earth to solve without carting around in outer space?
Well, I happen to be on the side of those who believe it's worth it to find out something we don't already know. You never know when even the most unimportant piece of information today may come in handy tomorrow.
Few people would have imagined that the micro-circuitry necessary for manned space travel would have been applied so quickly here on Earth in medicine, business, communications.
It occurs to me that Queen Isabella might well have been uninterested in whether the world was round or not, and stiffed Columbus.
Even so, somebody would have found out.
There are many things to learn in space.
And if we don't go looking for it, sooner or later, somebody else will.

April 27, 1981.
I can hardly wait for October.
That's when we get back the hour that the government took away from us this past weekend.
I know, an hour isn't all that much, but somehow I never feel that way in the spring and it takes me several days to adjust. I very carefully wander around the house and reset all the clocks, knowing full well that there's one somewhere that I will forget about that will send me off to work, or to an appointment an hour early one day soon.
Or is it an hour late?
I can figure it out; I just don't like to carry all these doubts around with me, I have quite enough doubts about other things that I can't figure out.
I know there's a very good purpose for Daylight Saving Time. It's supposed to save daylight. But I do at least half of my work at night, or used to, way back last week.
Ed Brauer wrote me last week and enclosed an article

123

from *Modern Maturity* which explains the origin of Daylight Saving Time.

It was an idea generated by an Indian chief whose feet stuck out from under the cover; so he cut off one end of the blanket and sewed it to the other end.

Ed didn't mention whether it worked or not.

May 6, 1981.

There was a letter in the Washington *Post* today that sorta hit home with me. It's probably going to make somebody angry, but I'm gonna talk about it anyway.

The writer is a historian named Marilyn Larew, who quotes another historian, Robert Dykstra. Larew says she's tired of hearing Americans blame their love affair with the handgun on the frontier experience.

She notes that Dodge City, the real Dodge City, had a total of just fifteen homicides during the height of its days as a cattle town, and that all the cattle towns in Kansas reported just forty-five homicides in the years between 1870 and 1885.

I don't know if it had anything to do with it or not but Kansas had a law in those days making it illegal for anyone other than a law officer to carry any dangerous weapon, concealed or otherwise.

Anyway, the point of this isn't to debate gun control, but to take the frontier off the hook. Apparently, our forebears didn't make a hobby of running around drawing on each other.

I guess the murderers of the Old West got themselves written about so much, and often so inaccurately because they were so rare, so unusual.

And the frontier people—just good and not so good folks that didn't have a very good press agent.

July 27, 1981.

The London newspapers are all upset.

It seems Nancy Reagan didn't curtsy when she met the queen. She just shook hands.

And, says Nancy, she won't curtsy again when she meets the queen again. She'll just shake hands.

Oh, that made the British newshounds mad.

"Nancy won't curtsy to the queen," read one headline.

"I won't bow, says Nancy," read another.

The *Daily Sun* was so bent out of shape about Mrs.

Reagan's refusal to curtsy that it ran a two-page story.

They would have run more but Lady Diana got upset with the photographers and cried at a polo match where Prince Charles was playing, and they had to save some space for that.

Anyway, the question of whether or not Nancy should have laid on a bow or a curtsy when she met the queen livened up what might have been an otherwise dull day for the British papers.

It didn't bother the queen at all, apparently. She's pretty used to Americans, I guess.

After all, a few years ago Louis Armstrong played a command performance at which he announced, "This is for you queen baby."

He got invited back and I bet Nancy will, too.

July 29, 1981.

I must confess, I kept telling myself for days that I would pay as little attention as possible to the royal wedding.

I am, after all, an American, and we decided two hundred years ago that we didn't hold with royalty.

Some of the presidents we've had, and not a few of the senators and congressmen forget that from time to time, and we have to remind them at the ballot box. But by and large we all agree that our leaders shall be either elected or appointed by somebody who is elected.

Anyway, in spite of my democratic, and I'd better add, republican leanings, I watched the wedding.

And, the pageantry was all I expected it to be.

I especially liked the trips to and from the church with all the horses, and carriages, and guards dressed to the teeth. I was terribly afraid that someone among the thousands on hand would step on Diana's dress.

But it was nice to know that both the prince and princess were capable of bobbling their lines, just like ordinary folk.

I noticed that our network anchor people bobbled some of their lines, too; and they're just ordinary folk. Heck, some of them are paid no better than a common prince or princess.

August 11, 1981.

I had a flat today, a very expensive flat, since the nail I found with a nearly new radial tire was long enough and bent in such a clever way that it was able to penetrate not only the tread of said expensive radial but also to engineer a tear in the sidewall of said expensive radial, rendering said expensive radial not worth repairing.

But that's not my complaint.

It's the first flat I've had in several years, and the odds were bound to catch up sooner or later.

My complaint is with the tire tools on modern cars.

My tire tools nestle, snugly and neatly along, and around, and under my spare. It's all very nice; they don't take up much room, or rattle the way they used to in my youth.

But, once one removes those tire tools and that spare from the trunk of the car, and changes one's flat with them, there is no way to get those same tire tools and the repaired tire into the trunk the way they were before.

The jack, you'll notice, is always six or eight inches longer than it was when you took it out; the single-armed combination hubcap bender and lug wrench, which is too long to remove the nuts without raising the car on a crane first, has mysteriously changed shape and will not fit into the groove you took it out of.

So, tonight, my tire tools rattle around in the trunk, the way they used to, and I could almost enjoy it—if radials weren't so expensive.

August 31, 1981.

The first day of school....

What visions that brings to mind, of the icy fear that can grip one's very soul at the idea of having to break in a new teacher, of entire bookfuls of learning that one has never seen before, of being seated at the front of the room where the teacher will always call on you first, especially if you don't know the answer.

It's been a long time, but I remember those fears very well.

What irritates me is that my daughter doesn't seem to have those fears, or to know what I'm talking about when I mention them. Her fear is that she may not be dressed exactly like the other girls in her class.

For weeks now Carolyn and her closest friend Christine have been planning their school wardrobes. The way it works—if Christine talked her folks into a certain item, then the pressure was on at our house for an identical item, and vice versa.

So, when the two of them trooped off to school this morning they were dressed identically...and their schoolmates, I later noticed, were pretty much wearing the same outfits.

If you have school-aged children, I'll give odds that the same sort of thing is happening at your house.

But, if you want to be made to feel that you just winged in from outer space, suggest uniforms....

Uniforms, never; after all, we're individuals.

CHAPTER 9

I have been of the opinion, for some time, that we have altogether too many holidays.

However, if I were given the power to cull out the needless ones, I'd be pretty nearly stopped. I like them all. All, that is, except the congressionally-approved Washington's Birthday on the third Monday of February.

If they had chosen the fourth Monday, we'd have one chance in seven of having Washington's Birthday on February 22, which is the actual birthday. The 22nd of February cannot, by any calendrical trick, ever occur on the third Monday.

Enough! Let us cherish and enjoy our holidays, content with the knowledge that they come, when Congress doesn't meddle....

BUT ONCE A YEAR

November 15, 1979.

I was skimming through a column on ideas for Christmas gifts today when one item caught my eye.

Diet soap.

You heard right, diet soap. Diet soap was developed by a couple of enterprising young businessmen in Maryland, and they've put it on the market now for $4.95 per bar.

They say it's all part of the "Fat Chance Diet Plan."

The idea is simple: diet soap takes off unwanted pounds safely and simply if you use it properly. You simply spend at least one mealtime a day in the shower or tub instead of at the table.

Just the thing for an overweight pet rock.

November 16, 1979.

And, if you're not interested in either crude oil or diet soap, a further suggestion.

By special arrangement with Joe Foulkes, I can now make available a limited supply of Tidewater weather.

This weather comes boxed, suitable for gift wrapping in tasteful cartons, and sells for ten dollars per cubic inch. Please order your weather early for Christmas giving, since supplies of certain varieties of weather may be limited.

With your order, please specify the particular type of

weather you prefer, and what time of day you want it collected.

Snow, sleet and hail are shipped in dehydrated form, and you simply add water and slip such weather into the refrigerator or freezer shortly before serving . . . . . .

We are, at present, having some technical problems with sunrises and sunsets, but hope to have them available to mix with our high quality weather by Valentines Day.

All orders for weather should be accompanied by a substantial quantity of cash, since we don't want to burden the Internal Revenue Service with a lot of extra bookkeeping at this busy season.

That's Thirteen News and a brazen attempt to capitalize on our position.

November 29, 1979.

One of the advantages of owning a farm is that you can harvest your own Christmas tree.

That's also one of the disadvantages.

Within five minutes walk from our farmhouse at Elam, we Kincaids have hundreds of young pines, cedars, all varieties, and among them, literally dozens that are just perfect in size and shape to be Christmas trees.

The only trouble is—three individual ideas of what is the perfect size and shape will be tilting for supremacy when the big hunt begins.

Personally, I prefer a moderate, sensible tree. . . one that can be strung with lights from floor level as step-ladders make me dizzy.

My wife prefers a size she calls sensible—I call it a seedling.

And our daughter believes that any tree that doesn't plaster its top three feet against the ceiling is much too puny.

Based on past experience, and the blue-eyed negotiating skill of our ten-year-old, I can safely predict that we'll compromise, and cut the one she chooses.

December 3, 1979.

There's a fellow over in Charlottesville who's touting a new organization called SCROOGE. And, as the name implies, he's got some really strange ideas on Christmas.

The principles of SCROOGE, the Society to Curtail Ridiculous Outrageous and Ostentatious Gift Exchanges, are

129

clearly a danger to Christmas.

Oh, they'd keep some of the trappings...decorated trees, gifts for kids and such. But the competition, the fight to find something new and expensive, the traditional going-into-debt, would be gone.

Langen and his SCROOGE Society suggest home-style Christmases. Handwritten notes to friends and relatives, visits during the season to the poor, and lonely, and the elderly and the sick.

Just imagine if everyone did that sort of thing at Christmas?

Just imagine....

December 11, 1979.

Apparently those who heard our offer for boxed Tidewater weather were skeptical, and though we've had some inquiries, most of our potential customers seem to have concluded that we're trying to sell nothing for something.

Consider then, the offer being made by the Jaycees of Pensacola, Florida.

They're selling invisible goldfish.

Not only that, but invisible fishfood as well with which to feed your invisible goldfish.

I must admit, the Jaycees added a feature to their sales campaign that we didn't have in our boxed weather offer.

If you get your invisible goldfish home and find it isn't satisfactory, just bring it back and they'll exchange it for another...invisible goldfish.

December 18, 1979.

All those swans aswimming, no doubt reminded you as it did me, of the traditional song, "The Twelve Days of Christmas."

Now there's a Christmas past for you.

Seven swans aswimming, according to a researcher in Pittsburgh, would run over seven hundred dollars.

Five golden rings...out of the question.

As for eleven pipers piping and twelve drummers drumming, the fellows at the Musicians Local here in Norfolk tell me that would run about three hundred sixty dollars for a fifteen-minute performance of drumming and piping.

The lords aleaping would be a problem at any price; and the ladies dancing as well, since we've been short of hereditary

nobility in this country for some time.
 And the partridge in a pear tree... a clear violation of the game laws.
 How about a gift certificate for ten gallons of gasoline?

December 26, 1979.
 I have to report to you tonight on an ideal Christmas.
 We spent it on the farm.
 The firewood was dry and the fireplace started on the first try.
 Everything among the presents we exchanged fit properly, was the right color, needed no elaborate sets of easy-to-follow directions for instant assembly; and, if batteries were required, the batteries were there and the right size.
 It took less than half a day to find the perfect Christmas tree, less than half an hour to get it standing reasonably straight, and with the whole family pitching in, less than two hours to untangle the light strings.
 I hope yours was just as nice.

January 1, 1980.
 A story has come to my attention on the predictions of the soothsayers in Japan who have just ushered in the year of the monkey.
 They say this year will see turmoil, some food problems, an easing of the oil situation, economic upheavals, and more trouble for the dollar.
 But the thing that troubled me most in the story was the description of how the Japanese mark the new year. They toll their bells 108 times; once, they say, for each of man's passionate sins... not all sins, mind you, just the passionate ones, 108 of them.
 And I come away from that bit of information feeling that I must have missed something.

January 2, 1980.
 The story with which we closed this news broadcast last night, generated some curiosity. I got some calls today.
 The concern was about a mention that the Japanese usher in the new year by tolling a temple bell 108 times, once for each of man's passionate sins.
 The story didn't say what all those sins are, just that there are 108 of them.

I did some research, but nowhere could I find a listing of 108 sins, passionate or otherwise.

So, I went to Joe Foulkes, figuring that he's got enough miles on him to know at least part of the answer.

But Joe disappointed me; said he could think offhand of only around seventy.

January 1, 1980.

My good friend Guy Friddell reported in the *Virginian-Pilot* today that the coming decade looks pretty good.

He says we'll get older, wealthier, and maybe wiser here in the Old Dominion.

Elsewhere in my reading today, I ran across other positive news.

Not one single person was stopped for drunken driving in Petersburg, Hopewell, Colonial Heights, or in the counties of Dinwiddie or Prince George; and such activity was very light all over Tidewater.

Score one for Guy Friddell. We must have gotten wiser already.

Since he's right about that one, I expect to get older and richer any day now.

February 14, 1980.

As a special Valentine's Day salute to our audience, I'm about to demonstrate why I never took up poetry as an occupation.

    Roses are red and violets are blue.
    I think you're terrific, Brad Face thinks so too.
Joe Foulkes sends his love and wants you to know
If it were all up to him, you'd never have snow,
Except just at Christmas and New Year's and such,
And then just enough, and never too much.
And if I had my way, all the news would be good...
Politicians would speak so they could be understood;
And all of our crises, from Iran to pollution
Would have a quick, easy, and simple solution.
But we're stuck with the facts, and all we can say
Is, we hope that you're having one whale of a day....

February 14, 1980.

Those of you who were watching our early evening broadcast may remember that I closed with a little Valentine poem.

Well, critical acclaim has been flowing in all evening, and I thought I might report the early results.

Fourteen callers asked me to promise never to do it again.

Brad and Joe, in a burst of literary generosity, want me to announce that they had nothing whatever to do with the poem. I get full credit.

And a mover and shaker high in the ranks of the Republican Party called and asked me if I would consider running for public office.

As a Democrat.

July 3, 1980.

No less a man than John Adams was an advocate of fireworks as a proper manner of celebrating our nation's independence.

Of course he wanted that event celebrated on July 2, when the Continental Congress actually took the step; but, even on the fourth, if it had to be, I believe John Adams would have still been in favor of fireworks.

It's about the only thing I can find to disagree with John Adams about.

I have this prejudice against all loud noises, but most especially, explosive loud noises. The backfiring of a truck can spoil my whole afternoon. I love everything about the 1812 Overture but the cannons.

So, I'll rejoice in America's Independence tomorrow with a fervent wish that John Adams had been a fan of something quiet—like Viennese waltzes.

July 4, 1980.

In an effort to find some original way of saying "Happy Birthday to us," I spent much of the day reading in *Bartlett's Quotations* for something inspiring from one of the founders.

I expected Adams, or Jefferson, or Washington to supply a quote. And I did find some nice ones.

But the one I finally settled on, I ran across quite by accident. It's a quote that did more to arouse a surge of patriotism in me than about anything I'd read lately: and it was made by one of the founding fathers of the Soviet Union.

"It is true," said Lenin, "that liberty is precious; so precious that it must be rationed...."

How would you like to see him try to sell that idea to Patrick Henry, or Martin Luther King?

October 8, 1980.

Today, in case you haven't consulted your calendar, is Leif Ericson Day; and then three days from now it's Columbus Day, and we're bound to hear the same set of arguments all over again.

There are those who favor the Columbus story, 1492 and the Ocean Blue and all that. And then there are those who go with the Vikings several centuries earlier. Then lately there was that report that it may have been the Chinese who sailed here first.

Fred Harris, the former senator from Oklahoma, believes it might have been the Phoenicians who discovered America; but then Fred also thought he had a chance to be elected President back in '76.

But Fred's wife, Ladonna, who is running for Vice President this year on Barry Commoner's ticket, once talked with me about this matter of who discovered America.

Ladonna Harris is an Indian.

She says her ancestors were on this continent for thousands of years and knew where they were all along—and didn't need discovering in the first place.

November 11, 1980.

They used to call this day Armistice Day; in fact, I think there are two or three states where that's still the case.

It originally celebrated the end of World War I.

Of course, they didn't know it was World War I back then, it was simply the Great War, the war to end all wars.

Since then, we've had a good many more wars.

The second World War, Korea, Vietnam, even the Cold War, and each of those wars required our citizens to fight, or serve, or simply stand at the ready.

It's those who wore the country's uniform we celebrate today, all of them who went away from the warmth of their homes and families to do whatever it was that had to be done, as effectively as possible, and whether they really wanted to or not.

December 31, 1980.

Here we are just a few hours away from the new year and it occurred to me, while we were putting together this broadcast, that I've made no new year's resolutions.

I usually do make resolutions; but, unlike a lot of people, I make resolutions that I can keep. For instance, I resolved many years ago never to get hooked on rutabaga.

My producer says that's a silly resolution, that there's no evidence that rutabaga is habit forming; and even if it were, there's no reason to believe that it would be harmful.

I counter with the argument that rutabaga is merely one of those substances that the surgeon general has not yet looked into; and when he does, based on his past record, he'll almost certainly find out that rutabaga causes some sort of unpleasant reactions in laboratory rats.

So, I guess I'll renew my resolution to abstain totally from rutabaga.

I know that may call down the wrath of the rutabaga lobby on my head, but I'll just have to take that chance.

December 31, 1980.

If you're watching this news broadcast right now—and can make out what I'm saying—you obviously don't need a lot of advice about the perils of over celebrating on this last gasp of the year and decade.

But, if you're not presently in the same house where you intend to spend the night, and have a drive of anything more than a quarter of a mile ahead of you, please remember that this is amateur night.

It's a night on which many normally stable individuals feel entitled, even obligated, to act as if there were no tomorrow.

In some cases, sadly, they turn out to be right.

So, look out for the other type, enjoy and have a happy new year...the whole year.

CHAPTER 10

I feel left out sometimes when the subject turns to sports. Especially individual sports. Sports like jogging or racquetball or tennis. Some of my friends participate in such sports, and swear that they enjoy them.

I don't believe it! I think they're secretly trying to stay healthy, and just don't care to admit it.

My favorite sport is lying in the shade on a summer day. After several hours of this I am worn to a frazzle. After all, shade moves, and, depending on the size of the tree providing the shade, it's sometimes necessary to move several times. And when it does come time to move to shadier territory, a decision must be made.

Whether 'tis nobler...

TO SAUNTER OR TO AMBLE

December 19, 1979.

Being one of those people who doesn't believe in putting off until tomorrow anything that can be put off indefinitely, I have always considered myself a prime candidate for the National Procrastination Society.

However, I've never gotten around to filing an application.

Anyway, along about this time of year I always feel guilty about all the letters I've received during the year, and have neglected to answer.

I can't answer them all in the space of time allotted here, but I thought it might be well to answer at least one question that occurs in my mail with some frequency.

People ask, quite often, if I am a Democrat or a Republican.

The answer is yes.

July 17, 1980.

It's not going to come as news to anyone that the heat wave is here, and it's hard to take. But there are some blessings.

It's a perfect excuse not to jog.

Personally, I never started jogging in the first place, but I do know numbers of people who do. And try as I may, I can't get them to see the folly of their ways.

Tennis is good in hot weather—watched on television in an airconditioned room.

And I think crossword puzzles make sense.

But jogging, especially in weather like we're having now, is hazardous to one's health, and I'm sure the government will soon declare it so.

Just as soon as they can figure out where to print the label.

July 21, 1980.

I guess you've heard by now that the heat may be with us until September, so we might as well prepare to deal with it.

A number of hot weather hints have surfaced in the past few days, some of them quite workable.

Our forebears, of course, found plain hand-operated paper fans helpful, and I can give them high marks if for no other reason than they may remind you of how rough things were before air conditioning.

For those without air conditioning, I recommend a cool bath or shower.

For those who must work outside I recommend loose, light-colored clothing, a hat, plenty of liquids, and a careful eye on one's salt intake.

And for joggers and tennis players, I recommend a psychiatrist.

August 13, 1980.

I'm really depressed by this most recent medical theory, that a little bit of fat is probably good for you.

Here's the problem, I'm skinny, I've always been skinny, and best of all, skinny for free.

I don't engage in any regular program of exercise, I certainly don't jog, it's too expensive. What with all the special shoes you need, the high fashion jogging togs, the books, and the clubs you have to join, you know, to really call yourself a jogger.

So, being naturally skinny I've been getting a great deal of good out of sitting around watching ice cubes melt, knowing that thousands of my fellow citizens are taking a great deal of time, trouble and expense getting that way. And along comes this meddler, a Dr. Ansel Keys, and tells a nutritional conference that he's been studying the problem, and his studies show that it's probably best to be ten or twenty pounds overweight.

Obviously, I have to start overeating—and that's even more expensive than jogging..

August 22, 1980.
This is the day the art of sauntering is celebrated on Macinac Island, Michigan.

Now, you notice, I referred to sauntering as an art unlike jogging, or its cousin, running, which are classified as sports.

Even walking, when done for a purpose, can be good for you, and thus can be called a sport, or at least, a recreation.

Sauntering, which consists of moving leisurely about on foot, with no good purpose in mind, is not easy.

My wife often accuses me of sauntering to the refrigerator for ice cubes during our weekends at Elam. But that's not sauntering at all, that's moseying; and the trip from there to the cabinet is a definite amble and resembles a saunter only to the extent that a hurricane resembles a whirlwind.

No, sauntering is what you do after the glass is filled... preferably in the direction of a country sunset. And the way to perfection—practice, practice, practice.

September 5, 1980.
Today, in case you haven't been paying attention, is "Be Late for Something Day."

It's altogether possible that you didn't know there was such a thing as Be Late For Something Day; but there is, and has been for some years.

It's just that the Procrastinator's Club of America, which founded the day, never got around to mentioning it before. Or possibly, as a person who intends one day to join the club, I have neglected to read up on its bylaws and customs.

Something like that.

I'll look into it someday.

Anyway, celebrating Be Late For Something Day is very simple, and I'll have complete instructions on the matter for you, sometime, if I can get around to it.

September 12, 1980.
A few days ago when I got a "round tuit" in the mail, all my excuses for not doing things when they need doing melted like butter on a freshly-boiled ear of Silver Queen corn.

All the things I'd been promising my wife I'd do to the house, or the garden at Elam when I get "a round tuit," I now will be under extraordinary pressure to do.

A "tuit" of any shape is hard to live with; but a round one is the worst of all. And I wish that friendly and helpful viewer had kept the "tuit."

It puts a dedicated procrastinator like myself in serious danger of compromising his principles, and actually proceeding to do something today that could be put off until tomorrow.

I know there's a way out, there always is, ask any politician.

So, I think I'll take up a position on the porch swing at Elam this weekend and figure out what it is.

September 16, 1980.

I think I've finally figured out the problem of understanding between men and women.

It's simple. Men and women may look at the same thing, under the same conditions, and see something altogether different.

Take football for example. On a weekend afternoon, I see football as a gallant contest of will, strength, and cunning—a battle royal with no political considerations to take the fun out of it.

My wife, on the other hand, sees a silly game with a lot of oversized simpletons running around tripping each other.

On Monday nights I tend to agree with her.

But it goes further....

At Elam, my wife looks at the outside walls of our old farmhouse and sees cracked and peeling paint. I see a venerable old structure that bears testimony to the summers and winters it has served as shelter from the forces of nature.

Especially so on a weekend afternoon.

October 14, 1980.

I had a letter today from a concerned viewer. He was complimentary about our news staff, but unhappy with our newsdesk.

Says it looks like a casket.

Says every time he watches our program he has the feeling the whole set is missing the bronze handles and the other three pallbearers.

Says he likes our newscast on the whole, but every time he tunes in and gets a good look at our desk he feels something like he's attending the memorial for a dear friend.

Well Herb, the way the news goes some nights, I get the same feeling, and I understand.
It's sorta like watching the Redskins play football.

July 27, 1981.

This being a Monday night, if there were no baseball strike I would not be speaking to you right now; I would be waiting for the Monday Night Baseball game to end.

Just about now Howard Cosell would be telling us about a particular triple play he had witnessed some years ago, or how much this particular game reminded him of the third game of the 1948 World Series.

That's reason enough in itself to continue the strike. But it seems the players and the owners have no trouble at all coming up with sufficient other reasons to continue to be disagreeable.

Personally, I think they've waited too long. There's going to be a football game next Saturday.

And what if baseball fans are like some of us are about smoking?

Heck, if I could quit for forty-six days I believe I could quit for good.

But I think the big mistake the baseball folks have made is one of proving that their loyalty, that is their real dedication to baseball, is based on the amount of money to be gained.

The strike puts to rest all the old rumors about sportsmanship, and the game, and giving the fans a good show being of importance.

What if, just what if, the strike ends and the fans go on strike?

July 30, 1981.

It was interesting to note today the various versions of the real reasons behind President Reagan's tax cut victory in the House of Representatives yesterday.

Those on the winning side of the question saw the vote as a result of an intense lobbying effort by the White House.

The losers saw it as the result of intense political arm twisting.

The letters, mailgrams, and phone calls to members of Congress were either the voice of the American people making itself heard, or a carefully orchestrated campaign by special interest pressure groups.

And the result of the vote will be, again depending on which side you're on, either a new era of prosperity or an economic disaster.

Later on last night after the business of the day and most of the extreme statements had been made, Speaker O'Neill called the President and congratulated him and called him "old pal." And the President agreed that he and Tip are good friends after six.

Then there was the annual ball game between the Democrats and the Republicans. The Republicans won that one, too.

Strangely enough, most agreed that the President's men won the ball game because they played better.

It occurred to me that that might be what happened in the House, too. I don't know, but it could've happened that way.

July 31, 1981.
I grew up, like most Americans, with an almost mystic attachment to the game of baseball.

Like most, I played the game when I was a youngster.

The ball might be held together with electrical tape, and the bat might be just a fairly straight limb off a tree, and there might never be enough gloves to go around, but baseball was our game. It belonged to us.

Baseball players were the majority then.

You needed to be fairly big and strong to play football, fairly tall to play basketball, but all baseball required was hustle, and enough kids on hand to choose up sides.

We never cared much for polo.

Polo was a game for the very rich. And while there's nothing wrong with being very rich, we just never got comfortable with polo. It was out of our league.

Well, the baseball strike is settled now. And before long they'll be playing again.

Somebody said the fans are the real winners. But I wonder.

I used to think of those players down there on the diamond as good old boys, playing their hearts out for team and hometown.

Now I know better.

Before long we'll be staying up late again for Monday

Night Baseball.
For all I care, they might as well play Monday Night Polo.

August 10, 1981.
I promised myself that I wouldn't do it. But, I've lied to myself before, and I did it again.
I tuned in to the all-star game last night.
I didn't watch much of tonight's Monday Night Baseball, but maybe that was because I was working. But I did tune in to part of the all-star game on the theory that I might never have the opportunity to see such a gathering of the wealthy again.
Imagine, as the all-stars, we were looking at the best paid performers in a profession that pays its average players over a hundred fifty thousand dollars a year.
Don't get me wrong, I have nothing against riches. Given the opportunity to put as high a price on my services as a baseball player, I'd do it in a minute.
And then I'd take part of that money straight to a charm school where I would be taught, no doubt, that it is unseemly for a rich man to spit, scratch, an adjust his underwear in public.

August 27, 1981.
As I've mentioned before, I don't care for jogging.
I know it's supposed to be good for your health, but I believe that's just a rumor circulated by people who make all the paraphernalia you have to have to jog properly.
I remember when it all got started.
All you had to do was go out somewhere and run; maybe in an old pair of sneakers and a sweat suit.
But now that it's the thing to do, you can't be seen on the street unless you have designer shoes, designer shorts and sweat suits, a stereophonic tape recorder, and electronic devices that deal with your heart rate, bio-rythms, and for all I know, your income tax bracket.
When John Glenn made the first space orbit back in the early sixties, he wasn't as well equipped as today's jogger!
And there are books on jogging, magazines on jogging, jogging schools, jogging clubs, and bumper stickers that joggers put on their cars so that people will know that they're riding, but under protest.
I sit in a porch swing for exercise at Elam. Sometimes I

even swing, but never very much. And I don't recommend it for everyone.
If word gets around it'll be a fad and I won't be able to afford it.

September 14, 1981.
Over the weekend I had the good fortune to be a guest at a combination pig-picking and pool party. One of these is an old southern tradition, and one isn't, but it was a grand affair.
Anyway, I decided to make the most of a natural disinclination on my part to take any sort of violent exercise unless it's absolutely necessary. And not even then if I can get someone else to do it.
So, I equipped myself with my pipe and a generous portion of a certain product distributed by the heirs of a certain Mister Daniel who used to live in Lynchburg, Tennessee.
Then, I set myself adrift in the pool on one of these rubber mattress affairs, basking in the sun, taking an occasional puff on my pipe and an occasional sip, and contemplating the glories of nature whenever one happened to swim by.
Little did I know that a plot was afoot.
All at once my reverie was interrupted by a shout, and the spectre of a certain television executive and a certain television engineer hurtling through the air in my direction.
Their purpose, they later said, was scientific. They wanted to explore the mental processes of TV anchormen and see, if swamped, whether they prioritize tobacco or spirits.
I could have saved them the trouble. You can always dry out a pipe.

September 17, 1981.
I was wrong about the Leonard-Hearnes fight.
For one thing, I thought Hearnes would win, and said so in the hearing of witnesses. And I thought the fight would go the distance, that it would be a decision.
I believed Hearnes would win on the basis of a feeling that a young man who is not yet a millionaire would fight harder to be a millionaire than would a fighter who is already a millionaire and was certain to get more millions either way the fight came out.
Don't get me wrong, I'm not disappointed at the outcome.
I would have a hard time feeling sorry for either of the fighters after a contest in which both were assured of coming

out rich no matter who won.

Just imagine, for forty-five minutes of fist fighting—good fist fighting—both these young men earned many times what the President of the United States will earn in four years, or even eight years, win or lose.

But it's nothing new.

Way back in the twenties a baseball player named Babe Ruth made more than the President. Then it was unusual and somebody asked the Babe if he didn't feel bad about it.

"Why should I," said the Bambino, "I had a better year than the President."

Thus far, so have Hearnes and Leonard.

October 26, 1981.

I don't like Mondays. I never have liked Mondays. And even though I didn't like Mondays back before Monday Night Football, I like Mondays even less now that there is Monday Night Football.

I realize that it's risky to make an admission like that to an audience that probably wouldn't be up this time of night if it didn't like football, but I hasten to add that it's not football I dislike, it's Monday Night Football in particular.

Football belongs in its place.

Friday nights for high schools.

Saturday afternoons for college.

And Sundays and holidays for the pro.

That's the natural order of things.

I realize, some very bright and highly-paid executives at ABC thought up the idea, and who am I to second guess them.

Well sir, just remember that those are the same guys who think that Howard Cosell knows something about grammar.

Isn't it just possible that they're also wrong about Monday Night Football?

CHAPTER 11

Tidewater and my farm at Elam have only one major unovercomable fault. That being that they are where they are, one hundred fifty miles apart.

If Elam were located somewhere in Suffolk, or York, or if Tidewater were closer to Pamplin City or Tuggle, everything would be perfect. But they're not, and I love both too dearly to give up either one of them.

So, five days a week I'm home in Tidewater, and the other two, I'm home at Elam, and thus am happy seven days a week.

The wonderful thing about it is that if I'm at either end, or on my way from one to the other, I'm solidly...

DOWN HOME

November 6, 1979.

Well, you know by now about the monumental foulup with some of our voting machines. Seems Norfolk voting officials simply forgot to unlock them.

I guess that's understandable...election days coming about so seldom and all.

The Democrats, of course, say it was a plot by the Republicans.

Republicans have been heard to mutter that it was skulduggery by the Democrats.

I don't know, I only know that no one has been arrested so far.

It's probably unjust, but the whole affair does call to mind an observation by the great American humorist and political observer Will Rogers.

He said, as near as I can remember, more men have been elected between sundown and sunup than have been elected between sunup and sundown.

November 6, 1979.

It's mostly over now, and those who will represent us in Richmond have been chosen.

If your candidate won, our congratulations.

If your candidate lost, our sympathy.

The nice thing about our system is that, win or lose, we

have the right to complain long and loud about almost anything they do while in office.

And we will.

And that's one of the more charming things about democracy that infuriates politicians and keeps journalists working steady.

November 27, 1979.
Science is wonderful.

A few days ago we found out that the universe is only half as old as we thought it was.

Then today, scientists told of discovering some footprints in an ancient African lakeshore.

Said those footprints are one and a half million years old, were made by an individual who was walking from a muddy area into a less muddy area, and that that individual was between five and five-and-a-half feet tall, and weighed about 120 pounds.

All that information from one and a half million years ago.

So, how come we still don't know for sure who won the Norfolk-Virginia Beach Senate race twenty days ago?

January 17, 1980.

I do sympathize with our highway officials—all those roads to build and no money to do it with.

I know they're worried about it and looking for some answers.

Just last November, as a matter of fact, four high-level Virginia officials attended a conference of road contractors.

The Virginia Roadbuilders' Association, in a rare stroke of logic, held the meeting over the course of a week...in Hawaii.

Those top-level officials, convinced no doubt that they could learn something about Virginia roadbuilding in Hawaii, that they couldn't learn in Virginia, assure us that they were able to talk over a broad range of problems with the contractors.

I don't suppose you'd like to take a wild guess at who paid the bill?

February 7, 1980.

Earlier this evening, I commented on yesterday's decision by Tidewater area school officials to close schools, at the regular time, in the face of what a great many people thought was the threat of a major snowstorm.

During the course of the evening, I received a goodly number of calls, many of them from teachers, agreeing with me that the decision was delayed far beyond the time when it could have headed off a great deal of worry and discomfort.

One caller, however, thought I was unfair, noting that Joe Foulkes was also caught by the weather—which seems on the face of it a very good point.

Indeed, Joe conscientiously went to the weather instruments at the airport and developed further information based on them and his own knowledge of weather patterns.

Indeed the weather, or rather the traffic jam caused by the weather, made it impossible for him to get here.

He did, however, get the information here, as he did night before last when he told us the storm was coming.

Joe got caught by the weather all right.

But he got caught *doing* his job.

April 10, 1980.
I have a faithful viewer in Newport News. I don't know if it's a man or a woman, but I do know this viewer pays attention.

The letters are always unsigned but friendly, literate, and helpful.

In the past I've been put straight on the pronunciation of Tidewater names, corrected on the use of certain words and phrases, such as Daylight Savings Time when it should be Daylight Saving Time.

However, the information on Daylight Saving Time was incomplete; it's nice to be able to pronounce it properly, but I still don't know for sure which direction to set the clock when it comes around.

But I digress.

In the most recent letter from my correspondent in Newport News I found an error and my joy was complete.

Virginia does not now, nor has it ever had a Governor name Miles Goodwin.

August 1, 1980.
You may remember that we reported last week on the purchase of a tent by the State of Virginia.

147

It was Governor Dalton who ordered the tent, a large canopy-type affair that could be used for outdoor receptions.

And, being suspicious sorts, some members of the media noted that Governor Dalton seemed to notice the need for a tent at just about the same point in time a reception was being planned for his daughter's wedding at the Governor's mansion.

Anyway, the Governor announced today that he will pay for the tent with his own money, expressing regrets that folks connected the tent purchase with the wedding reception, thus embarrassing his family.

He still thinks the state needs a tent, and should have a tent for other occasions, but he also wants his daughter's wedding to be as happy as possible.

I'm sure we all join him in that wish.

May 7, 1981.
I see in the *Ledger-Star* today that the new Mills E. Godwin, Jr. Bridge over the Nansemond River is going to open tomorrow.

It'll be a wonderful thing for the travelers along Route 17.

They won't have to wait for boat traffic to pass under a draw span any more.

It's a wonderful thing for former Governor Godwin, too. Here he is getting monumental structures named after him while he's still around to appreciate the glory of it all.

I've met Governor Godwin. Luckily I met him after I'd been in Virginia long enough to learn that his name is Mills Godwin, and not Miles Goodwin; and that he was, in the opinion of people I know in both parties, a fine and effective governor, both times.

Probably could be again if he wanted to....

But he doesn't want to.

He told me so himself.

And if I were going to name a bridge after a great Virginian, Governor Godwin would be one of the first I'd choose.

It'd be sort of a dead heat between Governor Godwin, Thomas Jefferson, and Mookie Wilson.

Jefferson's already had a lot of things named after him. Mookie would probably be more comfortable with his name on a candy bar. So Governor Godwin was the obvious choice.

I'm glad for him and I'm glad for those folks who won't

have to wait for the drawbridge, too.
Even the drawbridge tenders, who'll lose their jobs in this modernization, will be reassigned, according to the Highway Department.
I love happy endings.

June 3, 1981.

You may recall me mentioning last week that I had a letter from Gloucester bemoaning the fact that grocery stores no longer carry chicken necks, and that this fact is leading to a dreadful, and perhaps final, decline in the ancient and honorable art of chicken necking for crabs.

Well sir, Upshur Joyner has written me from Poquoson about a book that may shed some light on the problem.

According to Mister Joyner, William W. Warner's book "Beautiful Swimmers" is all about watermen, crabs, and the Chesapeake Bay.

And in that book Warner quotes a fellow named Lester Lee, who is a commercial crabber, and should know something about catching the delicious little rascals.

Lester says that anybody in his right mind knows full well that cut up eel is the proper bait for crabs, and allows as how those who use chicken necks are mostly high level civil servants from Washington, D.C. who have weekend places on the Eastern Shore.

I must admit that I have never been crabbing with either chicken necks or with cut up eel.

In fact I have never crabbed at all; but I've eaten a lot of them and I believe that crabbing is worthwhile.

And, I'll try to stay on top of this controversy till a solution is found.

Television is, after all a powerful medium—and if we can't address the burning issues of the day, what good are we?

July 15, 1981.

Have you heard about the big expedition in Chesapeake?
They're looking for Bigfoot out in the Northwest River Park.

According to the Associated Press there are several folks who have spotted a big, hairy, smelly creature. And some are convinced that it's the legendary creature that crops up from time to time and is known by various names like Bigfoot, Sasquatch, and in Asia, as the Abominable Snowman.

149

I have to admit that I've never seen a Bigfoot, nor have I seen the Loch Ness Monster, or a flying saucer. But in spite of all that I'm sure they're real.

But if there is a Bigfoot in Chesapeake, I sorta hope they don't find it. If it's really as smelly as some of the witnesses say, they'll want to give it a bath and civilize it. And if it's as tall as they say, about eight feet, somebody's going to come along and offer it a basketball contract.

If Bigfoot really wanted anything to do with us, he'd probably have come out and howdied and shook with us by now.

Bigfoot offers us, as long as he's free, a sense of adventure and mystery.

All we have to offer him would be modern society, zip codes, social security numbers, inflation, income taxes, and so on.

It's not a fair swap.

July 24, 1981.

I had dinner last night with the Fraternal Order of Police Associates, a gathering of businessmen whose purpose is to promote and appreciate quality police work.

It's sorta like the dog bites man, man bites dog syndrome.

If a policeman does his job badly, that's news; if he does it well, you probably won't hear about that.

Anyway, it was a grand evening, with speeches by the founder of the Norfolk Lodge, Herman Kline, and Tony Scarangella, a mover and shaker in the organization for years.

But the real stars of the evening were two young men: The Police Officer of the Quarter was Steve Watts. Unless you're family, or a friend, you probably never heard of Steve Watts, mainly because he's one of those officers, and there are many, who do their jobs well.

Then there was Dennis Jones. Dennis Jones saw a fellow man arrested, tried, and convicted of a crime Jones believed he had not committed.

He didn't stop till he proved it—and cleared the man's name.

It's a dangerous world out there; but just imagine how much more dangerous it would be without the work done by people like Watts and Jones.

There's no blaze of gunfire, or dramatic chase in this

police story.
Maybe it isn't even news, but isn't it nice to know?

CHAPTER 12

This old passion of mine for looking back at times past could probably be better served in a museum, but I prefer Elam. It's more personal.

When I contemplate a two-hundred-year-old log wall I can imagine the generations of people who did the same. I believe, and have good reason to, that they had vegetables in the garden, and dogs in the yard, and carried wood in to this same fireplace in winter, and savored the sweet water from this same well in summer.

And I believe they spent some time as I do, looking back and....

LOOKING AHEAD

January 31, 1980.

I should have seen this coming.

Yesterday I noted that I might celebrate groundhog day on my farm at Elam by watching for a groundhog that lives near my garden.

This particular groundhog harvested my sweet corn last summer, among other things from my garden, and I hinted that if my aim is good, we might have an early spring.

Sure enough, a ground hog lover called and made me feel about three inches tall.

So, I guess the Elam groundhog is safe for the moment.

But this year he's going to have to plant his own sweet corn.

March 20, 1980.

I've mentioned from time to time my troubles with a certain groundhog that takes it upon himself to harvest my sweet corn before I do.

And, I'm happy to report, the public response has been gratifying.

I've been deluged with all sorts of recipes for preparing groundhog, suggestions for methods of making the groundhog feel unwelcome, and offers from several hunters in the area to go personally to Elam and cure my groundhog problem once and for all.

However, I'm now faced with an added problem.

If I kill, cook, or evict that groundhog, what am I going to do for comment material on a slow day?

April 28, 1980.
Here's confirmation of what some of us have suspected for a long time.
Pets are good for you.
The dean of veterinary medicine at Washington State University says loneliness can be as serious as an illness, and that one of the best and surest cures for loneliness is a pet.
Says it works on loneliness like chicken soup works on a cold.
And, except for some of the obvious drawbacks, like paper training, pets have no serious side effects. The good doctor says scientific studies show that pet owners are happier than non-pet owners.
That's not earth-shaking news, of course, but isn't it nice to know?

May 21, 1980.
My family's garden is out in the country where there's plenty of room, so we plant a large one. But I was interested to see on the Associated Press wire today that a ten by ten foot plot is plenty of garden for a family of four.
The article was about urban gardening, a relatively recent resurgence of what we called "victory gardens" back in World War II.
I'm going to resist the heavy temptation to give out gardening tips; what works for me, in my soil, might be the wrongest thing you could do; but I do have to pass one on from Cornell University.
According to the professorial voice of Cornell you need the following elements for a garden: Light, nutrients, supporting media, water, and optimum temperature.
He left out the part about hard labor, but you'll find out about that anyway.

June 23, 1980.
In this space last Friday, Jane Gardner concluded a week of filling in for me with a note to the effect that the makers of Jack Daniel's sour mash whiskey have been enjoying an unusual degree of prosperity in this part of Virginia.
I read Jane's remarks carefully, and concluded that she

might, just possibly, have been attributing part of that success to my presence here.

While I will admit to an occasional sip for medicinal purposes, I hardly think that constitutes a large measure of sour mash consumption.

Now, at Elam, on the other hand, we do have an inordinate number of rattlesnakes and one owes it to oneself to be prepared.

June 30, 1980.

According to tradition, the dog days of summer are not really scheduled to start for several days; but I have to report that the dogs of Elam started early this year.

Saturday, and yesterday, I spent most of my time sitting in the shadiest spot I could find. And, I couldn't help but notice that my dogs did the same thing.

They did make occasional trips to the creek that runs through our backyard to commune with the ducks and lie belly down in the cold water.

During the weekend, when I was there, I felt a kinship for those dogs. We were all in the same boat.

But this is Monday, and they're there, on the banks or in the waters of an ice cold spring-fed creek; and I'm here, wearing a necktie.

I don't think, under the circumstances, that envy is an unreasonable emotion.

July 8, 1980.

The crops and garden vegetables I planted this year at Elam are not doing too well because of the dry weather; but I'm happy to report that the blackberries, which were there when I got there, and will probably be there when I'm gone, are flourishing.

There are several excellent patches of blackberries, including one where I encountered a nest of yellow jacket wasps last blackberry season.

This weekend I ventured forth to pick enough blackberries for a cobbler, and I thought about that particular patch.

I found that I know the general location of many patches of blackberries, the approximate location of others, but the one that belongs to those yellow jackets, I've got the location of that one down solid.

July 14, 1980.

A tornado, or something very much like a tornado, passed through Elam last Thursday, and our family has spent most of the daylight hours since then cleaning up after it.

I'm happy to report that the damage was mostly minor and repairable, a few sheets of roofing that left with the storm and lots of free firewood all around....

I guess the major loss, one we'll feel for a long time, was an ancient mulberry tree in the front yard.

It was mostly down and across the porch roof and the remainder looks a little forlorn and lopsided.

It is, however, in the opinion of my eleven-year-old, the best climbing tree in Virginia.

I hope we can save it.

It takes a long time to grow a good climbing tree.

August 8, 1980.

I've had a number of phone calls and letters lately inquiring as to the location of Elam.

I really don't understand the confusion, since I go there every Friday night, and I always find it on the first try.

Anyway, it's not in North Carolina. At least not the Elam where my farm is located. It is, in fact, in some of the prettiest country the State of Virginia affords, and you know how pretty that is.

But I realize that is somewhat confusing, so I'll describe the location of Elam once more for those who missed it the last time I dealt with this controversy.

Elam is about halfway between Pamplin City and Tuggle.

August 14, 1980.

When my wife and I bought the farm at Elam some years ago, we had visions of raising much of our own food there.

The way we figured it, it might not be any less expensive, but we'd know where it came from and that it was quality stuff.

So, we populated the place with, among other things, ducks and chickens.

Enter Carolyn, our eleven-year-old.

Anything that moves, she names it, and it immediately becomes ineligible for the cooking pot.

We have growing flocks of ducks and chickens, and if I

even mention their readiness for the table I am regarded as a latter day Attila about to sack Rome.
We've called off plans to raise a steer for beef.
Who needs a pet that weighs a ton?

September 1, 1980.
I had a couple of calls recently from people who were interested in how our garden at Elam turned out this year.
Well, during vacation last week I had a chance to assess things. And they could be better. The sweet corn, that the groundhog ate last year, fell victim to the dry weather.
This year the groundhog is having to make do with my field corn, which is so-so, but he's having to share it with the deer.
We did have a little wet spell a few weeks back, and the soybeans and some tomato plants hung in there for a small crop.
The terrapins liked the tomatoes very much.
But, we're back to dry weather at Elam again and last week about the only thing that grew really well was my hair.
I plan to have it harvested tomorrow.

November 27, 1980.
Last night I regaled that hardy lot of viewers who stay up late with the tale of my weekend, and my attempts to stay on the upwind side of my dog who had a close encounter of the worst kind with a skunk.
Today, no less than a dozen viewers have called in to pass the word that the only way to cure a dog of this malady is with generous quantities of tomato juice.
I already knew about the rumor, but the only tomato juice I had on hand had already been mixed with vodka and adorned with a twist of lime.
But I decided, what the heck, it might still work.
The dog drank half and I drank the other half.
The dog still smelled to high heavens, but neither of us minded as much.

May 7, 1981.
In the mail today were several inquiries about my Irish setter Murphy and how he's faring on the farm at Elam.
One writer complained of not being brought up to date on Murphy lately; and another sent him an aerial map of Elam,

in my care, which I appreciate since it does confirm the existence of Elam.

So, in the face of another attack of jealousy on the part of Joe's dog Ahab, here's a Murphy report.

Murphy is prospering.

He's given up chasing ducks, cars and chickens completely; he still chases an occasional cat, but he hasn't caught one yet and they like to climb trees anyway.

He loves to chase rabbits and, considering their appetite for garden peas, we have not tried to discourage this habit.

I'm sorry to report that Murphy was feeling poorly last week.

Our vet, Doc Taylor, said he had tonsillitis, gave us some pills and told us to give Murphy chicken soup. Murphy wasn't too thrilled about the pills, but he took them, and he liked the idea of the chicken soup just fine.

He liked it so well, in fact, that he snuck into the kitchen and appropriated a chicken that had been programmed as a family dinner.

We didn't discover the theft until too late. But it was nice to know that Murphy had his appetite back.

May 21, 1981.

I was made to feel a little better about the herd of dogs we have at Elam today. We have four, all sort of rescued in one way or another.

Fifi was found abandoned at a service station by a friend who realized immediately that we needed just such a dog.

Spanky was adopted when another friend promised one of her friends to find Spanky a home. Stranger just showed up one day several years ago and never got around to leaving.

And Murphy, our Irish setter, was adopted after another friend took pictures of him at the shelter.

We buy dog food in fifty-pound bags.

Anyway, Chet Riddick, one of our engineers, was driving me out to Suffolk today to speak to the Rotary Club. But first we had to drop by his house to see Benjy.

Seems Chet got Benjy sort of the same way I got my bunch.

This friend had a friend who was about to move away and couldn't take Benjy, and would Chet take him. And Chet, being a nice guy, and an animal lover, and having several acres around his house for Benjy to share with his other dogs... well, sure, after all we all know that Benjies are fuzzy little dogs about so high, seen 'em on television.

Well sir, this particularly Benjy is fuzzy all right, and lovable, all one hundred eighty-five pounds of him.

Who'd ever guess that anybody would name a St. Bernard Benjy?

June 3, 1981.

Bettie Watkins of Virginia Beach wrote today to ask if the birds of Elam are reasonable creatures.

It seems Bettie's birds in Virginia Beach are not reasonable at all; and in the matter of cherries they're no more willing to compromise than the National Rifle Association.

Bettie says she'd be willing to let the birds harvest one side of the tree and leave her the other, or maybe work out a shared time arrangement. But her birds make only one concession to the fact that it is, after all, Bettie's cherry tree: they take the red cherries and leave her the green ones.

Oh, they do occasionally pick a red cherry and drop it on the ground; but those always turn out to be inhabited by a worm.

Bettie says she can't figure that one out because birds are supposed to like worms just as much as they like cherries.

It could be, I suppose, that Bettie's birds are so grateful to her for providing them with a cherry tree that they save the very best ones for her.

I don't know if I've correctly probed the thinking of these birds or not, but some of my colleagues have suggested that I'm as qualified for that mission as anybody they know.

July 16, 1981.

I consider myself one of the more fortunate news broadcasters I know.

If you're a regular viewer you know that I like to talk about my farm at Elam and that management allows me to do that. And another thing I enjoy is getting mail from viewers with comments and questions about Elam and the various experiences we have there.

Today I got a letter from Clyde Harris who described the picture he's built up in his mind over the past couple of years.

Clyde sees me sitting on a columned portico, gazing out over a greensward contentedly, contemplatively, even cogitatively, with a mint julep in my hand.

Clyde says that's how he wishes Elam to be.

And Clyde's vision is close in some respects. The mint julep is usually a Jack Daniels, the greensward often needs mowing, and the portico is what some less romantic types might call a porch. But in the essentials Clyde and I see Elam the same way—and it's going to be that way if it takes twenty years.

And when I get it that way, I'm going to look Clyde up and invite him to come to Elam and sit on my portico and contemplate and cogitate with me.

I know just where there's a fine patch of mint for the juleps.

August 14, 1981.

It's been some time since I've rendered a progress report on my Irish setter, Murphy; but that's largely because there was nothing significant to report.

Also, because every time I mention Murphy, Joe makes another mark on his little ledge on the desk to remind me of all the publicity Murphy gets, and that his Dalmation, Ahab, doesn't get.

Anyway, if you'll remember, it took us quite a while to break Murphy of his habit of chasing things. Unlike Dalmatians, which specialize in chasing fire trucks, Murphy chased anything that would run from him, or for that matter anything that seemed to be running from him.

Murphy spent a lot of time in solitary those first few months; but we finally got him to give up chasing cars, trucks, ducks, and most cats.

His training seemed to hold up till a few days ago when a church meeting broke up about a mile from the farm—and the cars of the faithful started coming by in great numbers.

Well folks, Murphy fell off the wagon; such abundance was more than he could stand and before he could be caught and jailed, he chased them all: the old and the late model, the economy jobs, and the gas guzzlers.

Murphy indicated later on that he was truly sorry; but I suspect it was a term in solitary that he was sorry about.

September 3, 1981.

The roof of our old farmhouse at Elam needs painting, needs it badly. And I've made plans to do that this week. So naturally, the forecast is for rain.

The one consolation in that is that I'll be able to check to see if the tarring of that roof that I did last weekend did any good.

I don't know if you've ever tarred an ancient tin roof before. But in case you ever need to—take my advice and hire someone to do it.

For one thing, roofs are always steeper when you get on them than they look from the ground. For another, the holes are never where you think they're supposed to be.

I have carefully spotted all the leaks in the roof at Elam, know just where they are; I've put pans under all of them many times. But, observing from above, I find no holes or split seams whatever over those leaks.

I don't know what causes things to work out that way.

I suppose it's part of the same set of physical phenomena that causes my pipes to freeze when everyone else is talking about what a mild winter we're having.

But, I'm just borrowing trouble talking about frozen pipes.

That usually doesn't happen at Elam until after Labor Day.

September 3, 1981.

The fact that Pungo's resident Irish setter Dooley specializes in turning over garbage cans doesn't surprise me a bit.

Irish setters always specialize in something we'd rather they not do—and get away with it because they are beautiful, and loveable, and have no sense of guilt at all.

I suspect that Dooley is much like our Irish setter, Murphy, who beautifies the landscape at Elam when he's not busy wrecking it.

I don't know what Murphy is doing at this moment, but I do know the nature of what Murphy is doing.

He's probably digging a hole.

Some dogs dig in order to capture a mole, or a groundhog, or to bury a bone. Irish setters dig holes because there is not currently a hole there.

Or, possibly, Murphy is redistributing a compost pile in the garden, or proving once again that the trash receptacle has not been invented that an Irish setter can't get the lid off of.

Or, he's teaching ducks to fly, or cats to climb trees.

A friend of mine suggested that I send Murphy to an obedience school. Well, I would, but the folks at the Virginia Beach SPCA told me that Murphy has already been to obedience school.
And it was the truth, I know. I got a good look at the diploma shortly before Murphy ate it.

September 7, 1981.
We had plans to use all or part of this Labor Day weekend to put a new coat of paint on the old tin roof of our house at Elam.
Well, it rained all weekend at Elam; so, we weren't able to do that. But we were able to determine the location of several leaks in that roof. Well not the exact location. But we were able to determine that there are some leaks in locations other than the leaks we patched last weekend.
Whether these are new leaks or not, we still don't know. It could be that they are merely new manifestations of old leaks. This is to say, that some of the old leaks may not have taken to our patch job, but may be siphoning water from the roof to the inside of the house by new routes in order to fool us.
There is, for example, a leak in the downstairs hall well inside the house, but no leak whatever in the hall immediately above it.
A friend of ours suggested a new roof. I said I like tin roofs. He said they make a fiberglass roofing material that looks exactly like tin.
Trouble is, it doesn't sound like tin when it rains.
If you've ever slept under a tin roof during a summer rain—you know that a little leak here and there doesn't really make all that much difference.

September 10, 1981.
I've mentioned before that my dog Murphy, an Irish setter, had some bad habits when he came to live at Elam; mainly that he liked to chase things.
Well, he settled down considerably, but he still has an occasional relapse.
Some of the cats of Elam have never been fully convinced that Murphy has mended his ways, and they still run when they spot him, usually for the nearest tree, and Murphy obliges them by giving chase.
Murphy no longer chases cars at all, that is, cars in

general. He still chases one particular truck and an occasional funeral procession. But Murphy isn't the sort of dog to give up old favorite bad habits without replacing them with new and imaginative bad habits.

His latest passion is screen doors.

There's something about a screen door that offends Murphy; particularly a screen door that leads into a kitchen where there might be an unattended chicken or a roast, or a cake, or anything else that a large Irish setter might find appetizing.

So, we are running short of screen doors at Elam.

We have several screen door frames.

It's almost time to put the storm panes in those doors anyway, but I'm reasonably certain Murphy will feel about them the same way he feels about screen doors.

September 15, 1981.

Earlier on this broadcast we mentioned that it looks like a hard winter ahead, especially with regard to snow.

But I'd bet against it.

For one thing, my friend Luther and I spent a lot of very hot days in the woods during the spring and summer cutting wood for this winter.

And, as a result, I have a woodshed fully packed to the rafters with good, well-seasoned firewood. The chimneys of Elam are clean and in good condition. And the woodstoves and fireplaces are all in good working order.

These facts alone are enough to convince me that there's a mild winter ahead.

The only thing that holds me back from making a solid prediction of a mild winter is the fact that I have still been unable to figure a way to get insulation around some of the water pipes without first disassembling the house itself.

The crawl space is too shallow, and the man who put down an oak floor nailed to chestnut logs with square cut nails meant for that floor to stay right where it is.

I haven't given up hope just yet, and if I can find a way, we'll have that mild winter.

Nothing that I'm fully prepared to cope with ever happens.

I'll keep you posted.

October 20, 1981.

Joe Foulkes continues to complain that I have used this

time at the end of the program to praise the many talents of my Irish setter, Murphy, and completely neglected his Dalmatian, Ahab.

Well, I've always taken Joe's complaints with a grain of salt, because deep in my heart I had no intention of being unfair to Ahab; although Ahab has, on occasion been less than friendly towards me.

But now, I have to admit that maybe Joe's complaints have some validity. Perhaps I have talked too much about Murphy.

Since I have described, with great precision, the location of our farm at Elam several times over the past couple of years, the multitudes of visitors have been on the increase.

No less than three people have driven by and waved this year alone.

Anyway, it was last weekend that I was given to realize how much I had promoted Murphy. A family, obviously out for a summer drive, rode by while I was in the yard playing with Murphy.

I heard the driver say, "Look, there's Murphy, who's the guy with him?"

ACKNOWLEDGMENTS

It's very hard to know how to credit those legions of people one encounters in a lifetime... or even in a short space of that lifetime... and then to say, this one and that one helped me write this book... such as Catherine and Carolyn, the women in my life.

My mother, of course. Her retelling of some of the old family stories appears here, without nearly enough credit, especially in the form of Uncle Otto.

Then, there's Darrell McGraw, a Supreme Court Justice I once befriended in West Virginia, and who became very much a part of my life and of my storytelling.

There's Howard K. Smith, whom I admire so greatly, and who once praised my writing. But here I tread on dangerous ground, since I could never properly thank all my former colleagues at ABC and CBS for the encouragement they gave me, and the skills I stole from them in bits and pieces so no one would know. For these, I'll fall back on Harry Reasoner's copout in *Before The Colors Fade,* and blithely note that they know who they are.

Bob Friedman of Donning Company, for his faith, expert examination and, when possible, repair of my grammar. And the Halmais, Brigitte and Alex who helped and encouraged in ways difficult to explain, even to them.

Elam is so much a part of the book that I must acknowledge my debt to the old house, and the abundant land, and the refreshment it has provided.... And to Louise Foreman, who loved it even before we did, and to Chino and Faye Kearney, who leave the monuments of Washington behind as often as they can, and come to Elam to help us sing.

Colleagues at WVEC-TV have also been very supportive, especially my former producer, Bob Phelps, and my co-anchor, Jane Gardner.... Their daily readings of my comments, and offerings of advice, have been invaluable.

And finally, a special thank you to all who have ever said to me, "Jim, you ought to write a book." You know who you are....